THE

1950s

THE
1950s

Other books in this series:

THE
1950s

Stuart A. Kallen, *Book Editor*

David L. Bender, *Publisher*
Bruno Leone, *Executive Editor*
Bonnie Szumski, *Series Editor*
David M. Haugen, *Managing Editor*

Greenhaven Press, Inc., San Diego, California

AMERICA'S DECADES

Every effort has been made to trace the owners of copyrighted material. The articles in this volume may have been edited for content, length, and/or reading level. The titles have been changed to enhance the editorial purpose.

Library of Congress Cataloging-in-Publication Data

The 1950s / Stuart A. Kallen, book editor.
    p.   cm. — (America's decades)
    Includes bibliographical references and index.
    ISBN 0-7377-0304-0 (lib. bdg. : alk. paper) —
    ISBN 0-7377-0303-2 (pbk. : alk. paper)
    1. United States—Civilization—1945– . 2. Nineteen fifties. I. Kallen, Stuart A., 1955– . II. Series.

E169.12.A165 2000
973.92—dc21   99-047628
                                                         CIP

Cover photo: 1. Corbis/Bettmann 2. Corbis
JFK Library, 215
Library of Congress, 73, 115, 123, 129, 148, 165, 186
National Archives, 48, 98
Yale Collection of American Literature,
Beinecke Rare Book and Manuscript Library, 221

©2000 by Greenhaven Press, Inc.
P.O. Box 289009, San Diego, CA 92198-9009

Printed in the U.S.A.

Contents

Chapter 1: In the Shadow of the Cold War

1. The Superbomb and American Fears

by James T. Patterson   36
After the United States exploded the first hydrogen
bomb in 1952 the Soviet Union successfully tested its
own H-bomb. The fear of worldwide Communist domination swept through American society.

2. The Superpowers Go to War in Korea

by Arthur S. Link and William B. Catton   42
When Communist North Korea invaded South Korea
in 1950, the United States was drawn into a war that
no one wanted in a far-off land where a harsh climate
and rugged terrain made fighting extremely difficult. At
one point President Truman and his generals discussed
dropping nuclear weapons on Korea to win the war.

3. Building the Hydrogen Bomb *by Robert J. Donovan*   54

The United States was the only country in the world to
possess the atom bomb until the Soviet Union tested its
own A-bomb in 1949. Fearing the Soviets would use
the bomb in Europe, the U.S. government approved a
crash program to develop the hydrogen bomb, a device
one hundred times more powerful than the A-bomb.

4. A Soviet View of the Cold War

by Vladislav Zubok and Constantine Pleshakov   62
Though American domestic and foreign policy during
the cold war was largely open to debate, few people
knew what was happening inside the Soviet Union,
where secrecy was intrinsic to all government matters.
When the Soviet Union collapsed in the early 1990s,
cold war documents came to light that showed Soviet
leaders did not want to fight an all-out nuclear war

with the United States, but preferred to draw America into smaller proxy wars in other countries.

people reacted by building backyard bomb shelters in the ludicrous hope that they could survive a nuclear blast by moving their families into a hole in the ground lined with cinder block.

Chapter 3: The Racial Divide

1. The Death of Emmett Till

The Deep South was a dangerous place for African Americans in the 1950s. When a fourteen-year-old boy named Emmett Till, visiting Mississippi from Chicago, called a white woman "baby," he was dragged from his bed at night and murdered by men who were acquitted of the crime in the subsequent trial.

2. The Montgomery Bus Boycott

In Montgomery, Alabama, and in other southern states, black people were not allowed to ride in the same sections of public transportation as white people. When African American Rosa Parks refused to move to the back of a bus, she sparked the Montgomery bus boycott, which finally ended with integration of the city's buses.

3. High School Integration in Little Rock

School segregation was banned by the Supreme Court in 1954 and by 1957 Little Rock, Arkansas, was under court order to let black children attend the same schools as whites. When nine African American students attempted to integrate Central High in Little Rock, mobs of angry racists blocked their path, forcing the president to call out the army to guarantee the black children safe access to the high school.

Chapter 4: Suburban Culture in the Atomic Age

1. Moving to the Suburbs on the G.I. Bill

Between 1950 and 1960 over one-third of all Americans moved into newly built suburban neighborhoods. Many paid for their homes with low-interest loans provided by the G.I. Bill, comprehensive postwar legislation designed to reward veterans.

and William Burroughs founded the Beat movement that would later inspire a generation of sixties hippies.

Chapter 6: The Legacy of the 1950s

Foreword

In his book *The American Century*, historian Harold Evans maintains that the history of the twentieth century has been dominated by the rise of the United States as a global power: "The British dominated the nineteenth century, and the Chinese may cast a long shadow on the twenty-first, but the twentieth century belongs to the United States." In a 1998 interview he summarized his sweeping hypothesis this way: "At the beginning of the century the number of free democratic nations in the world was very limited. Now, at the end of the century, democracy is ascendant around the globe, and America has played the major part in making that happen."

As the new century dawns, historians are eager to appraise the past one hundred years. Evans's book is just one of many attempts to assess the historical impact that the United States has had in the past century. Although not all historians agree with Evans's characterization of the twentieth century as "America's century," no one disputes his basic observation that "in only the second century of its existence the United States became the world's leading economic, military and cultural power." For most of the twentieth century the United States has played an increasingly larger role in shaping world events. The Greenhaven Press America's Decades series is designed to help readers develop a better understanding of America and Americans during this important time.

Each volume in the ten-volume series provides an in-depth examination of the time period. In compiling each volume, editors have striven to cover not only the defining events of the decade—in both the domestic and international arenas—but also the cultural, intellectual, and technological trends that affected people's everyday lives.

Essays in the America's Decades series have been chosen for their concise, accessible, and engaging presentation of the facts. Each selection is preceded by a summary of the article's content. A comprehensive index and an annotated table of contents also aid readers in quickly locating material of interest. Each volume begins with an introductory essay that presents the broader themes of each decade. Several research aids are also present, including an extensive bibliography and a timeline that provides an at-a-glance overview of each decade.

Each volume in the Greenhaven Press America's Decades series serves as an informative introduction to a specific period in U.S. history. Together, the volumes comprise a detailed overview of twentieth century American history and serve as a valuable resource for students conducting research on this fascinating time period.

Introduction

The years from 1950 to 1960 have been characterized as a bland decade marked by cold war fears and suburban conformity. Though it is difficult to generalize about the lives of more than 170 million Americans during a ten-year period, it is true that the values of most Americans during that decade were forged by two pivotal events: the Great Depression of the 1930s and World War II in the 1940s. After twenty years marked by poverty, war, and the destruction of major European and Asian powers, conforming to the suburban way of life was a dream come true for Americans of the war generation.

African Americans, Asian Americans, Hispanics, and other minorities were not included in the American dream. Their lives were shaped by discrimination and poverty during the depression, segregation during the war, and continued segregation during the fifties. But these people had undergone the same collective experiences: They too fought in the war, and when it was over, began to expect equality and a share in the American dream.

It is easier for historians to discern the ebb and flow of human events in retrospect and identify broad causes and effects. Far more difficult is recognizing the consequences of people's actions as their lives unfold. Few could have predicted, therefore, the dominance of American culture by the postwar baby boomers reared in those idyllic 1950s suburbs. And few in the 1950s understood that hardhearted southern segregationists would spawn the civil rights movement leading to federal laws that guarantee equal rights not only to all minorities but to disabled people and other groups as well.

Although times change, people don't. The articles chosen for this anthology demonstrate that many issues confronting people fifty years ago are still relevant today. For instance, the world is still dealing with the consequences of the U.S.–Soviet nuclear arms race. Racial injustice still haunts America in hundreds of ways. And, of course, rock and roll music is in some ways as controversial today as it was then.

History, especially recent history, is subject to interpretation and revision, a puzzle from which the world we live in today was assembled. From *I Love Lucy* reruns to the Rock and Roll Hall of Fame, to the Martin Luther King holiday, to the concerns of aging baby boomers, the ideals, troubles, and good times of the monochrome fifties demand Americans' attention in the twenty-first century.

The 1950s: A Decade of Divergence

Looking back on the 1950s through a wide lens, the decade appears to be a time of relative harmony, especially in comparison with the wartime 1940s and the turbulent 1960s. In the fifties, divorce numbers were low, the U.S. economy was booming, and millions of Americans began raising families in newly built suburbia.

But like the black-and-white photographs, movies, and TV shows from that era, the fifties was a time of stark contrasts. On one hand, the U.S. economy was booming. Millions of optimistic, mostly male, single-wage earners were supporting families, buying houses and new cars, and sending their kids to college. On the other hand, the United States and the Soviet Union were engaged in what many saw as a reckless arms race, with both countries stockpiling enough hydrogen bombs to destroy the world twenty times over.

The contrasts were also evident in the social mores of the day. The fear of world Communist takeover spawned public suspicion and rejection of anything that was different or strange, reinforcing strict conformity of dress and manners in America. At the same time black rhythm-and-blues music merged with white country music to foment a rock-and-roll music rebellion. And while black roots music was popular among white teenagers, black people were denied equal rights and justice. In America's South, African Americans were forced to live in separate neighborhoods, attend separate schools, eat in separate restaurants, and sleep in separate hotels. In a booming postwar economy, average wages of African Americans were less than 50 percent those of whites.

Emergence of the Superpowers

America in the 1950s had recently emerged victorious from World War II, the most widespread and destructive war in history. This conflict killed over 50 million people and shattered the governments of European and Asian countries. The United States was spared the physical destruction of the war, but almost three hundred thousand Americans died in the conflict. With Europe rebuilding from the ruins, the United States emerged as the strongest and wealthiest country on earth—a world superpower for the first time.

When the bombs stopped falling in 1945, the world was a profoundly different place than it had been in 1939. The formerly powerful nations of Germany and Japan lay in ruins. America's ally in the war, the Soviet Union (USSR), suffered more than 20 million civilian and military casualties. But when the war ended the Communist giant emerged with the largest standing army in the world.

As a victor in World War II, the United States occupied Germany and other countries in Western Europe. The Soviet Union exerted its considerable influence in Eastern Europe. Before long Poland, Czechoslovakia, Hungary, Bulgaria, Romania, and others became Communist satellites under the control of Moscow.

The United States had ended the war with Japan by dropping atomic bombs on the cities of Hiroshima (population 300,000) and Nagasaki (population 250,000). Those two bombs killed at least 130,000 people and injured 110,000. Unfortunately for the United States, the secrets of the atom bomb soon fell into Soviet hands. Once in possession of the atom bomb, the USSR challenged the United States for world domination.

The two superpowers began a buildup of nuclear missiles at an unprecedented rate. In 1952, the United States began test explosions of hydrogen bombs (H-bombs) with one hundred times more destructive power than the atomic weapons dropped on Japan. A few months later, the Soviets exploded their own hydrogen bomb. The development of thermonuclear weapons led to a military stalemate between the competing superpowers known as the cold war.

Both countries believed that if one launched an attack, the other would instantly retaliate and nuclear annihilation would follow. Each stockpiled weapons for their deterrent value, a policy known as mutually assured destruction, or, appropriately, MAD. MAD forced the superpowers to enlist and support allies in Europe, Africa, Asia, and South America on economic and ideological terms. And each side loaded its military bases, ships, submarines, and airplanes with nuclear weapons just in case.

While fear of nuclear destruction increased in the general populace, it had an ironic side effect—the billions of dollars spent on the arms buildup was extremely beneficial to the U.S. economy.

Communist Expansion

Nuclear weapons were widely and immediately accepted by the popular press in the fifties. Magazines printed articles such as "Atomic Weapons Will Save Money." *Look* magazine cheerily pointed out that A-bombs were "one of the cheapest forms of destruction known to man."[1]

Average Americans also had strong opinions about atomic weapons. The general view was that the differences between the Soviet and American systems were irreconcilable. They were convinced that nuclear weaponry, once invented, would never go away. It was believed that the Soviets had less to lose and would launch a surprise attack on the United States. After wiping out North America, the Soviets would rule the world.

A Gallup poll taken in 1950 reflected this paranoia. Seventy percent of those surveyed believed the Soviet Union wanted to rule the world. Forty-one percent felt the United States would fight another war within five years. Seventy-five percent stated that they feared American cities would be bombed in the next war. Nineteen percent felt the next war, when it came, would wipe out the entire human race.

While Americans were pondering nuclear annihilation, half a world away, China fell to Mao Zedong's Communist government. After China became a Communist nation, more than one-quarter of the world's people—close to 500 million Chinese, and 220 million Soviets—lived under Communist rule. This terrified many Americans.

In 1950, North Korea invaded South Korea. The United States and other nations sent troops to defend the south, but after the Chinese intervened, the United States became enmeshed in a three-year war that no one would win.

For the majority of Americans simply trying to live their lives and raise families after the hardships of the depression in the 1930s and the horrors of World War II in the 1940s, superpower backing of regional conflicts was not reassuring.

The Red Scare at Home

With two of the world's largest countries living under the red flag of communism, Americans had good reasons to be fearful. Many believed it was only a matter of time before the Communists attempted to conquer the United States. And they projected their fears onto many of their fellow Americans.

Thousands of Americans had joined the Communist Party during the dark days of the Great Depression when massive unemployment caused many to become disenchanted with capitalism. These people became suspects in the fifties, even after they renounced Communist beliefs as youthful experimentation. Scientist and technicians who had worked on atomic bombs also came under suspicion when the Soviets developed their own weapons. Investigations exposing a handful of people as spies in fact convinced Americans that thousands more lived among them.

Many politicians—especially Republicans—took advantage of the "Red scare" to further their own political ends. These politicians accused President Truman, the Democrats, and liberals in general of being soft on communism. The truth was not a necessary factor in this Red-baiting, and one result was a massive Republican victory in the 1952 elections, with World War II general Dwight David Eisenhower elected president and the Republicans taking control of the House and Senate for the first time in decades.

Fear and hatred of Communists rose to a fever pitch. Many who did not fit into the status quo image of white, middle-class, Anglo-Saxon America were labeled "Commies." That included blacks fighting for equal rights, Jews, intellectuals, union organizers, immigrants, college professors, artists, musicians, poets, and others. Being branded with such a label could cause a person to lose his or her job, home, and, for recent immigrants, U.S. citizenship.

McCarthyism

The man leading the charge against suspected Communists was Wisconsin senator Joseph McCarthy. In February 1950, McCarthy delivered the following speech in West Virginia:

> While I cannot take the time to name all the men in the State Department who have been named as members of the Communist Party and members of a spy ring I have here in my hand a list of 205 that were known to the Secretary of State as being members of the Communist Party and who nevertheless are still working and shaping the policy of the State Department.[2]

The news services picked up this startling revelation and the speech made headlines the next day. McCarthy never showed his list to anyone; in fact, it was rumored to be his laundry list. But the fear-mongering and anti-Red hysteria of the so-called McCarthy era had begun.

McCarthy never proved his allegations against a single person, but for almost five years, his lies and slander disrupted the lives of all they touched. McCarthy conducted a personal vendetta against Hollywood and claimed more than two thousand actors, writers, directors, and producers were Communists. At institutions of higher learning, over six hundred professors were fired because of McCarthy. Public libraries were forced to remove books by or about Communists, Socialists, liberals, and even African Americans. Politicians from the city councils to the Senate were scrutinized.

To be labeled a Communist by McCarthy was tantamount to being called a traitor to one's country. At the time, it was one of the most ruinous of charges. People who were snared in McCarthy's web lost their jobs and their friends. Careers were ruined, marriages were destroyed, and families were torn apart.

Finally McCarthy took on a much more powerful opponent—the U.S. Army. It came to light that McCarthy had waged a campaign to get special treatment for his personal assistant, G. David Schine, as an army private. In the summer of 1954, the Senate launched the Army-McCarthy hearings to investigate the accusations against the senator. During the first-ever televised Senate hearings, millions of Americans saw McCarthy in action for the first time. When he attacked and slandered respected military officers, his popularity rapidly declined and his Red-baiting career was over. The Senate soon began an investigation into McCarthy's conduct as a senator that resulted in his official censure. Although he remained a senator, after the censure McCarthy was a broken man. He died in 1957.

The Racial Divide

While white Americans were worrying about Communists in the government, many black Americans were simply hoping for equal treatment under the law. When millions of white veterans returned home from World War II, they quickly moved into good jobs in a burgeoning economy. When African American soldiers returned, they faced the same racism and prejudice that had been thrust upon them before the war.

But things were changing in America, if slowly. In 1944, the National Association for the Advancement of Colored People (NAACP) won a long court fight to have white-only election primaries rendered illegal. (This allowed black people to vote in the South Carolina primaries for the first time since 1877.) In 1948, President Truman desegregated the military and Supreme Court decisions desegregated graduate schools in the South.

Still, the life of the average African American was not changed by these advances. When columnist Walter Winchell asked a young black woman in Harlem how Hitler should be punished for his war crimes she said:

"Paint him black and send him over here."[3]

African Americans had been living under a discriminatory policy known as "separate but equal" since 1896. That year, the Supreme Court said black people could be segregated from whites in schools and other places as long as the facilities were equal in quality. As a result, segregation ruled, but equality never came. In the South, states spent an average of ten times more money on schools for whites as they did on black schools. Most black schools were in run-down buildings with few books or supplies.

By the 1950s, a wide variety of laws prohibited African Americans from using white streetcars, restrooms, schools, parks, restaurants, water fountains, and other facilities. These so-called Jim Crow laws were generally enforced in the American South where blacks also faced discrimination in voting practices. Author Langston Hughes wrote, "Blacks who wanted to serve their country did so at the risk of their dignity and sometimes at the risk of their lives, long before they met the official enemy. The enemy that hurt them worst was Jim Crow. Jim Crow ignored their citizenship and scorned them as human beings."[4]

Court-Ordered Desegregation

On May 17, 1954, the Supreme Court ruled that the separate-but-equal doctrine was unconstitutional in public education. In its decision in the case *Brown v. Board of Education of Topeka, Kansas* the Court ruled that "To separate the Negro children from others of a similar age and qualifications solely because of their race generates a feeling of inferiority as to their status in the community that may affect their hearts and minds in a way unlikely ever to be undone."[5]

Two weeks later, the Court ordered all seventeen states with separate-but-equal schools to integrate them immediately. In 1955, the Court said the ruling also applied to tax-supported colleges and universities.

Brown v. Board of Education set off battles in the South unlike any since the Civil War. The governors of South Carolina, Georgia, and Mississippi threatened to abolish public schools before they would let blacks and whites attend classes together. One hundred senators and congressmen from the South signed a petition against the ruling. Racist hate groups formed to protest the decision. State, county, and city politicians drew up laws to circumvent the Supreme Court ruling. Random acts of violence by whites against blacks increased dramatically.

Early in 1957, the Eisenhower administration sent Congress a civil rights bill, the first of its kind in the twentieth century. In its original form, the measure provided for a Civil Rights Commission to investigate abuses against black people. It permitted the Department of Justice to intervene on behalf of those whose right to vote was denied in southern states. The bill passed the House of Representatives, but in the Senate, it ran headlong into the opposition of powerful southern senators.

In protest of the bill, Senator Strom Thurmond of South Carolina filibustered the chamber for a record-breaking twenty-four hours and nineteen minutes. The bill was finally passed in compromised form. It turned out to be mostly symbolic, because it left the Civil Rights Commission powerless and reduced the ability of the federal government to support black voting rights.

The Baby Boom

The fifties were marred by racism and the threat of nuclear annihilation, but many Americans floated through those years on a cloud of prosperity and family values. There was an emphasis on marriage, children, and family life during the decade. Men and women began to marry at an earlier age, at an average of twenty-two for men and nineteen for women. The divorce rate, which had risen slowly from the 1920s, leveled off at 10 percent. Divorce was stigmatized and considered socially unacceptable.

Before the fifties, due to housing shortages and economic hard times, children often grew up in the same house with grandparents, aunts, uncles, and other extended family members. But in the fifties, suburban "nuclear families" predominated, made up of a mother, father, and their children. These families did almost everything together. They went to church, went on vacation, saw ball games, worked in the yard, watched television, and washed the car. And they multiplied. Between 1946 and 1964, 30 million children were born—more than 4 million a year after the mid-1950s. (In 1957, one baby was born every 7 seconds in America.) This "baby boom" formed a huge demographic that influenced everything from the sale of diapers and cars to the popularity of rock and roll.

Booming Suburban Population

After the war, inexpensive, assembly-line housing sprang up on the East Coast and was soon imitated everywhere. Thousands of very similar houses crowded into instant suburbs built on the outskirts of big cities. Families could have modern appliances, individual bedrooms, garages, and lawns for as little as $6,000 in the late forties. Veterans used low-interest loans to snap up the houses, and the suburb boom was born.

The population of the United States jumped almost 30 million from 150.7 million in 1950 to 180 million in 1960, the largest increase for any decade in the country's history. Incredibly, 83 percent of this growth occurred in the newly built suburbs; by 1960, 60 million people, or one-third of the population, had moved to suburbs that had not even existed in 1950.

Most Americans who lived in the suburbs still worked in city centers. And the quality of their jobs was unprecedented. Labor unions were strong and collective bargaining secured workers the means to enter the middle class. Huge corporations paid white-collar workers very well. People expected to hold one job for their entire careers and retire at age sixty-two.

The Role of Women

In the years before women's liberation, fifties women were simply expected to perform the jobs of stay-at-home mothers. A widely read book titled *The Women's Guide to Better Living* advised, "The family is the unit to which you most genuinely belong. . . . The family is the center of your living. If it isn't, you've gone far astray."[6] The woman's basic need, it was said, was to be wife, mother, and homemaker. Her only means of completion and fulfillment was childbearing. TV personality Alan Ludden noted in one of his advice books that a teenage girl "knows that as a women she will be doing a great deal more for others than will be done for herself."[7] Writer Paul Landis said, "Except for the sick, the badly crippled, the deformed, the emotionally warped, and the mentally defective, almost everyone has an opportunity to marry."[8]

Many women said they were content to work at home for their husbands and families. Women also served society in other ways: They volunteered for charity drives, as Boy and Girl Scout den mothers, on boards of the Parent Teacher Associations, and taught Sunday school.

Teenage America

White suburban children of the postwar baby boom were the best-fed, best-educated, and best-cared-for generation in history. And the richest. As one commentator remarked in the mid-fifties, "Teen-agers of today, are stronger, smarter, more self-sufficient and more constructive than any other generation of teen-agers in history."[9] For the first time, teenagers were considered a unique demographic group, and advertisers paid attention.

In reality, fifties mass culture was dominated by business. And business expected people to indulge themselves with conspicuous consumption. Teens were no exception. In earlier times, when teenagers made money, their earnings went to support their parents, or the money was saved for one treasured item such as a bicycle, or for college tuition. But fifties teenagers, with no memory of the depression, had no instinct to save money. They became a brand-new consumer class.

Scholastic magazine showed that by 1956 there were 13

million teenagers in the country with a total income of $7 billion a year. This was 26 percent more than in 1953. The average teenager had an income of $10.55 a week, close to the average family's disposable income (after all bills were paid) in 1940. Teens spent it on TVs, phonographs, records, pimple cream, and lipstick (alone worth $20 million in 1958).

Television Nation

From exploding H-bombs to the hip-shaking Elvis Presley, Americans watched the images of the fifties flicker by on black-and-white television sets. The small-screened televisions in lacquered wooden boxes permanently changed how Americans saw the world, and how the world saw America.

Before 1945, television was a clumsy and expensive toy for the wealthy. But the wartime invention of the Image Orthicon "picture" tube made inexpensive television sets a reality. In 1946, only 7,000 TV sets existed in the United States. By 1950, 4.4 million families were tuning in to the wonders of television. By 1956 people were buying TV sets at the rate of twenty thousand a day. In 1960 Americans owned 50 million televisions and 90 percent of American homes had at least one TV.

Sales of televisions caused unexpected booms in the sale of other items. In 1955 alone, Americans bought 4 million new refrigerators. The reason? Frozen food. Old models generally had tiny freezers with room for only a few ice cube trays. New refrigerators were designed for a brand-new invention—TV dinners. The family sit-down dinner was replaced by consuming food from aluminum trays in front of the TV. Television changed the way people looked, acted, and consumed. This common invention was the most sudden and huge communication change in history.

The early days of TV are called the golden age of television. Since the first TV viewers were affluent people who regularly supported the arts, early programming included opera, live original dramas, re-creations of Broadway plays, high-quality documentaries, and variety shows along with the comedy, news, and adventure programming. Added to this mix was the fact that most TV in those days was broadcast live. It was immediate and authentic. Flubbed lines, accidents on the set, and stage fright added to the excitement of the shows.

Live TV also showed millions of people the workings of their government for the first time. This was best demonstrated during the Army-McCarthy hearings, broadcast live in 1954 and watched by millions. When Americans saw the unfair, bullying tactics of Senator McCarthy, his four-year reign of terror ended almost overnight.

But there was a negative side to television's message. Television functioned best when presenting simple stories in neat thirty-minute units. By the late fifties, TV portrayed an antiseptic world of idealized homes in an unflawed America. Shows like *Leave it to Beaver* and *Ozzie and Harriet* showcased families in which the father worked, the mother cooked and cleaned, and children got into the most minor mischief. On *Leave it to Beaver,* Ward Cleaver once asked his wife June, "What type of girl would you have Wally [their older son] marry?" "Oh," answered June. "Some very sensible girl from a nice family . . . one with both feet on the ground, who's a good cook, and can keep a nice house, and see that he's happy."[10]

There were no economic problems, no ethnic tensions, and few, if any, minority characters on television serials. Racial stereotypes were reinforced—southerners were portrayed as simple rustics in *The Real McCoys.* Blacks were portrayed as stuttering schemers in *The Amos and Andy Show.* Women were portrayed as impeccably dressed helpmates on shows like *Ozzie and Harriet.*

"Gotta Be Rock and Roll Music"

The wide acceptance of television affected the entire range of fifties arts and entertainment. From the falling popularity of movies to the rising popularity of rock and roll, television distracted and attracted people's ever-shortening attention spans. While TV was the centerpiece of fifties family life, another louder and more insistent beat was central to the lives of millions of teens. Rock music supplied a wild rainbow of color in an otherwise drab decade.

In the early 1950s, smoky rhythm-and-blues music (R&B) called "boogie-woogie" or "race music," emanated from African American radio stations. Gospel-tinged vocals called "doo-whop" were recorded with little or no instrumental backing.

In 1951 a white record store owner in Cleveland, Ohio, noticed white teens from the suburbs were buying R&B and doo-whop records by black artists. He told a local disc jockey named Alan Freed, who began to play some of the wild new records on *The Moondog Show,* Freed's fifty-thousand-watt clear-channel radio program. The station was so strong that *The Moondog Show* skipped across the stratosphere to a vast area of the Midwest. Teenagers could tune in from rural towns, big cities, and suburbs to hear Freed spinning records, chattering wildly, and beating on a Cleveland phone book with a drumstick. To millions of teens isolated in dull, conformist towns, this might as well have been music from outer space.

Freed described the music with a term from Wild Bill Moore's 1947 hit, *We're Gonna Rock, We're Gonna Roll.* Moondog's Rock and Roll Party became an instant success and made stars of black artists such as Fats Domino, Johnny Ace, Johnny Otis, the Drifters, the Platters, and the Moonglows. Before long millions of teenagers were buying the records of Elvis Presley, Little Richard, and others singing the Chuck Berry lyric "rock and roll will never die."

In the spring of 1955, MGM released the movie *The Blackboard Jungle* about a high school teacher confronted by violent students. The song on the opening credits was Bill Haley and the Comets' "Rock Around the Clock." It created a nationwide sensation. Overexcited teens caused riots in some theaters. The movie was called "degenerate," but Haley's song shot to number one and the rock era had begun. By the summer of 1955, the record had sold a million copies.

Rock Backlash

As the popularity of rock and roll continued to grow, so did opposition to the music. The so-called objectionable content of rock songs triggered fierce parental and religious campaigns against the songs. Rock music was banned from many radio stations. In some towns rock records were broken, piled up, and burned. "Smash the records you possess which present a pagan culture and pagan concept of life," urged the newspaper of the Catholic Youth Center. "Some songwriters need a good swift kick. So do some singers. So do some disc jockeys." Law-enforcement agencies banned rock and R&B concerts, especially those where blacks performed with whites on the same stage. In the South, White Citizens' Councils spoke out against "bop and savage Negro music." When Elvis performed at the Pan Pacific auditorium in Los Angeles, he was ordered to "clean up his show or else."[11]

Before long the Red-baiters in Congress found a new target. Congress decided to investigate the music industry and found that record companies paid disc jockeys bribes to play certain records. This practice, called payola, was common in the entire music industry at the time. Congress chose only to investigate rock-and-roll music. Alan Freed became the target of a payola investigation. Congressional investigators assumed that rock was "evil, ugly, unintelligible, and bad, and that teen-agers were passive victims who never would have listened to it unless it had been forced upon them by illegal activity."[12]

The Beat Generation

Although rock music got most of the attention, other types of music became popular in the fifties. History's greatest jazz legends were at their peak in the fifties. Miles Davis, Charlie Parker, Lester Young, Dizzy Gillespie, Dave Brubeck, and others could be found performing in jazz clubs in America's big cities. Their records sold in respectable numbers.

Jazz was popular among African Americans, but it was also the music of the so-called Beat generation. (*Beat* originally meant "cheated or emotionally drained" but was reinvented to mean "beatific" or at peace. The term was later expanded to beatnik. Before the term *Beat* came along, artistic nonconformists were called bohemians.)

The Beats came together over bottles of cheap wine and books of verse by Beat writers Allen Ginsberg, Lawrence Ferlinghetti, William Burroughs, and Jack Kerouac as well as French poets such as Flaubert, Baudelaire, and Rimbaud. They spoke of a New Vision—a society of artist-citizens in which they would be leaders. They recorded their thoughts and dreams on reams of paper.

Scientific Advances in the Nuclear Age

The Beats and rock-and-roll music were simply distractions to most Americans who were living in the most creative scientific era the world had ever known. The fifties were a time of many technological firsts. Scientists synthesized wonder drugs that ended a plague of diseases. They invented huge computers to unravel age-old mathematical problems in minutes. They created transistors that changed electronics, and the world, forever.

Using missile technology developed for military use, scientists launched communications satellites. With technology developed to build jet fighters, they built sleeker, faster cars and began cross-county passenger jet service. Even radioactive nuclear isotopes were put to peaceful uses in medicine and energy production.

Of course, this technology came with a price. Bigger cars clogged highways and polluted the air. Nuclear testing spread radioactivity across the land. New pesticides killed pests along with good insects, birds, fish, and even people. And the garbage from America's brand-new throwaway society piled up in junkyards and dumps from coast to coast.

To the average person in the fifties, however, it was a

miraculous age of discovery. New technology touched everyone. Children watching television were able to clock the countdowns of U.S. space flights. Common people discussed such nuclear concepts as fission and fusion. And the world rejoiced when modern medicine wiped out smallpox, yellow fever, and polio. Scientists, who had been thought of as absent-minded tinkerers, became the new heroes in postwar America.

Not only could chemical elements be used to produce power in nuclear reactions, they could be used to heal the sick as well. For the first time in the fifties, radioactive isotopes were used to diagnose disease and to treat cancer.

Perhaps no area of research experienced such a broad range of discovery during the fifties than medical science. The discovery of penicillin in 1941 saved untold lives during World War II. By the mid-1950s medical researchers had studied some 3,500 other antibiotics and had introduced seventeen for use in humans against rheumatic fever, pneumonia, and tuberculosis. Researchers also developed vaccines against a host of childhood illnesses such as measles.

Perhaps the greatest medical conquest was that over polio. By 1952 polio was killing more children than any other communicable disease. To combat this menace, the March of Dimes was formed. By the 1950s, it raised over $67 million a year to discover a cure for the disease. Over 100 million Americans contributed money to the March of Dimes every year.

This was the situation when a young medical doctor named Jonas Salk discovered a polio vaccine in 1954. On April 12, 1955, the vaccine was declared safe and effective. It was a victory for the entire country. By 1962, polio had been virtually eliminated. Only 910 cases were reported that year, down from 37,476 in 1954. Salk was rewarded with his own research institute in La Jolla, California.

Tailfins and Chrome

Modern medicine changed people's lives for the better. But there was no more potent symbol of the fifties than the automobile. Not only was the automobile changing lives, but it was changing the countryside as well. One of the most important events of the 1950s would forever alter the look and the pace of life in the United States. This was the federal National Defense Highway Act of 1956. This bill provided for the construction of forty-one thousand miles of freeways, to be built over a ten-year period, at a cost of $26 billion. The act was one of the largest public construction projects ever undertaken in the United States. And in the end, it lasted more than twenty-five years and cost over $100 billion.

The highways were necessary because of the record number of cars being built. From 1950 onward, more than 8 million cars were built every year. By 1958, almost 68 million cars and trucks were in use—more than one for every household in the United States. Total vehicle miles traveled jumped from 458 billion in 1950 to 800 billion in 1960. More suburbanites needed more cars to get to work in the cities and enjoy leisure travel, and the cars people drove guzzled more gas and spewed more pollution as they got longer and heavier.

It was oil that fueled the cars. During the war, vast new pipelines and great refineries were built to create easy access to America's vast domestic oil reserves. Oil consumption nearly doubled during the fifties. The era was marked by gas wars among filling stations, each fighting for customers by setting its prices a half-cent a gallon lower than the competitions.

Plastics and Pesticides

The glut of oil fueled a huge chemical industry whose motto was "Better Living Through Chemistry." Not only did oil feed cars and industry, but chemical magicians were creating a whole new world using plastics. These compounds, which were lightweight, malleable, and easy to produce, started showing up in all aspects of modern life. From brightly colored kitchen chairs to telephones to Elvis records, it was hard to remember the world of only a few years before where there was no plastic.

Plastic was not the only new chemical product making its way into American life. The chemical industry developed dozens of compounds that could be used as pesticides and herbicides. Use of these chemicals on farm crops increased tenfold.

Pesticides and fertilizers, along with modernized farm equipment, allowed people in the fifties to experience a "green revolution." Never before had so few farmers grown so much food for so many people. But as pesticide and herbicide use increased, insects and weeds developed resistance to the poisons necessitating new and heavier applications. Helpful animals and fish, along with rivers, lakes and streams, were fouled by pesticides.

Into the Sixties

In 1959, one establishment figure evaluating the youth of the fifties wrote about University of California students: "Employers are going to love this generation. They are going to be easy to handle. There aren't going to be any riots."[13] Even as he spoke, his predictions were proving false. The times were (as songwriter Bob Dylan would soon tell us) a-changin'.

Fifties practices such as nuclear testing, militarism, and compulsory military service began to stir students to active protest in the late fifties. Also during this time, unknown to most Americans, Ralph Nader was investigating auto safety and Rachel Carson was amassing evidence against the pesticide DDT. But the biggest change of the early sixties came on May 9, 1960, when the Food and Drug Administration quietly approved the first oral contraceptive for women—the birth control pill. The Pill quickly revolutionized relations between the sexes, freeing many women from the age-old fear of pregnancy. It set in motion a sexual revolution that still affects people today.

The end of the decade was the beginning of a long youth rebellion. Writer H. Stuart Bell wrote approvingly: "For the more imaginative and sensitive men and women under thirty, ideology and utopia are far from dead. They have suddenly and rather surprisingly come to life after ten blank years of slumber."[14]

From today's perspective we can look back and see that it was the baby boomers—raised in the fifties—who originated the modern environmental, women's, and civil rights movements. The world as we see it today can be traced back, on a rather crooked line, to that era known as the fifties.

1. Quoted in David Wright and Elly Petra Press, *America in the 20th Century, 1950–1959*. New York: Marshall Cavandish, p. 808.

2. Quoted in David Halberstam, *The Fifties*. New York: Villard, 1993, p. 50.

3. Quoted in Douglas T. Miller and Marion Nowak, *The Fifties: The Way We Really Were*. Garden City, NY: Doubleday, 1975, p. 183.

4. Quoted in Stuart A. Kallen, *The Civil Rights Movement*. Minneapolis, MN: Abdo & Daughters, 1990, p. 14.

5. Quoted in I.F. Stone, *The Haunted Fifties*. New York: Random House, 1969, p. 61.

6. Quoted in Miller and Nowak, *The Fifties*, p. 147.

7. Quoted in Miller and Nowak, *The Fifties*, p. 147.

8. Quoted in Miller and Nowak, *The Fifties*, p. 154.

9. Quoted in Miller and Nowak, *The Fifties*, p. 269.

10. Quoted in Halberstam, *The Fifties*, p. 509.

11. Quoted in Miller and Nowak, *The Fifties*, p. 307.

12. Quoted in Miller and Nowak, *The Fifties*, p. 308.

13. Quoted in Miller and Nowak, *The Fifties*, p. 395.

14. Quoted in Miller and Nowak, *The Fifties*, p. 398.

CHAPTER 1

In the Shadow of the Cold War

AMERICA'S DECADES

The Superbomb and American Fears

James T. Patterson

The explosion of the first hydrogen bomb in 1952 initiated more than a nuclear chain reaction. It also set into motion a chain reaction of fear and doubt throughout American society. With the awesome power to immolate the entire globe, and with the Soviet Union possessing the same capabilities, a wave of fear, paranoia, and anti-Communist hysteria descended upon American society. James T. Patterson is a Ford Foundation Professor of History at Brown University.

When Truman announced his decision [to build the superbomb], many liberals were appalled. [Journalist] Max Lerner wrote, "One of the great moral battles of our time has been lost. To move toward the ultimate weapon could mean only an ever-escalating arms race, the possible decay of democracy in a garrison atmosphere . . . and the possibilities of unimaginable horror." Other liberals, however, backed the President. [Historian] Arthur Schlesinger, Jr., replied to critics like Lerner by asking, "Does morality ever require a society to expose itself to the threat of absolute destruction?" Schlesinger's answer, of course, was no, as was Truman's. Given the frigid Cold War atmosphere of early 1950, the decision to go ahead with the hydrogen

Excerpted from *Grand Expectations: The United States 1945–1974*, by James T. Patterson. Copyright ©1996 by Oxford University Press, Inc. Reprinted with permission from the Oxford University Press, Inc.

bomb seems to have been virtually unavoidable.

Development, as it turned out, proved complicated, in part because of formidable mathematical problems involved. But scientists and mathematicians, including the strongly anti-Communist Hungarian refugees Edward Teller and John von Neumann, persisted. With the help of more powerful computers, which were becoming vitally important in the high-tech world of American weaponry, they moved rapidly ahead. The world's first thermonuclear explosion took place on November 1, 1952, at Eniwetok Atoll in the Marshall Islands of the Pacific.

The explosion exceeded all expectations, throwing off a fireball five miles high and four miles wide and a mushroom cloud twenty-five miles high and 1,200 miles wide. Eniwetok disappeared, replaced by a hole in the Pacific floor that was a mile long and 175 feet deep. Scientists figured that if the blast had been detonated over land, it would have vaporized cities the size of Washington and leveled all of New York City from Central Park to Washington Square.

Eight months later, on August 12, 1953, the Soviets followed suit, setting off a blast in Siberia. Premier Georgi Malenkov announced, "the United States no longer has a monopoly on the hydrogen bomb." His boast was somewhat misleading, for the Soviets (like the Americans) did not yet have the capacity to make a "bomb" light enough to be delivered on a target. Still, development raced ahead in the next few years, not only in the United States and the Soviet Union but also in other nations. The age of nuclear proliferation and of maximum possible destruction was near at hand.

The Super[bomb] represented one half of the plans in 1950 for America's future military posture. National Security Council Document 68 (NSC-68), which called for vast increases in defense spending, was the other. It, too had its roots in late January. Truman then authorized a study of defense policy and named Paul Nitze . . . as head of the State Department's Policy Planning Staff, to head the effort. . . . Another key adviser in the process that led to NSC-68 in April

was Robert Lovett, who later that year left his own investment banking business to return to government as the Deputy
Secretary of Defense.

"Death Comes Slowly"

Nitze, Lovett, and the others who worked on NSC-68 in
early 1950 were virtually fixated on the Soviet atomic explosion, and they adopted a worst-case scenario for the
world. Asserting that the USSR would have the capacity to
deliver 100 atomic weapons on the United States by 1954,
they rejected arguments that a moderate mix of economic,
military, political, and psychological measures would be
sufficient to contain the Soviet Union and keep major areas
of industrial-military value—mostly in western Europe—
out of hostile hands. They insisted instead that the Soviet
Union was an aggressive, implacable, and dangerous foe
that either directly or indirectly (by infiltration and intimidation) sought domination of the world. As Lovett put it in
an apocalyptic memo:

> We must realize that we are now in a mortal conflict; that
> we are now in a war worse than any we have experienced.
> Just because there is not much shooting as yet does not
> mean that we are in a cold war. It is not a cold war; it is a
> hot war. The only difference between this and previous wars
> is that death comes more slowly and in a different fashion.

The obvious conclusion was that the United States and
its allies must build up not only their nuclear power but
also their more conventional forces "to a point at which
the combined strength will be superior . . . to the forces
that can be brought to bear by the Soviet Union and its
satellites." This amounted to what was later called a policy
of "flexible response." Although the committee did not include cost estimates for this policy, advocates understood
that military spending would have to quadruple to around
$50 billion a year, which would "provide an adequate de-
fense against air attack on the United States and Canada
and an adequate defense against air and surface attack on

the United Kingdom and Western Europe, Alaska, the Western Pacific, Africa, and the Near and Middle East, and on long lines of communication to those areas."

This was a breathtaking and revolutionary document, full of emotional language contrasting the "slave society" of Communists to the blessings of the "Free World." The USSR, "unlike previous aspirants to hegemony, is animated by a new fanatic faith, antithetical to our own, and seeks to impose its absolute authority over the rest of the world." Soviet fanaticism necessitated globalistic responses: "The assault on free institutions is world-wide now, and in the context of the present polarization of power a defeat of free institutions anywhere is a defeat everywhere."

The conclusions of NSC-68 rested on one key assumption, which reflected the grand expectations that pervaded America in the postwar era: economic growth in the United States made such a huge expansion of defense spending easy to manage, and without major sacrifices at home. One of Lovett's memos strongly made this case: *There was practically nothing the country could not do if it wanted to do it.*. . . Then, as throughout in the postwar era, grand expectations about American economic and industrial growth promoted globalistic foreign and military policies.

Supported by All High-Ranking Officials

NSC-68 was seriously flawed in many respects. As Kennan complained at the time, it assumed the worst of Soviet foreign policy, which for the most part remained cautious, concentrating on tightening control of eastern Europe and other sensitive regions close to Soviet boundaries. NSC-68 also defined United States defense policies in terms of hypothetical Soviet moves rather than in terms of carefully defined American interests. This approach required the United States to be prepared to put out fires all over the globe.

The report's assumptions about the relationships between Soviet and American power were especially questionable. In 1949 the American GNP was roughly four times as great as that of the Soviet Union, which remained an inefficient and relatively unproductive society. Although the Soviets were devoting perhaps twice as much of their GNP to military spending, this was being done at terrific costs at home and could not make them serious economic rivals of the United States in the foreseeable future. The Soviets maintained a much bigger army, but they had used it to stamp out dissent in their spheres of interest, not to invade new territories. There was no clear indication in 1950 that this largely defensive posture would change. America had much the greater arsenal of nuclear weapons, by far the superior navy, much stronger allies, and incomparably greater economic health. As it turned out, moreover, the Soviets did not make a big effort to improve their long-range bombing forces until the mid-1950s; NSC's worries about nuclear attack as early as 1954 were way off the mark.

When Truman received the report in early April, he neither endorsed nor rejected it. Instead, he passed it along for economic analysis. If the Korean War had not broken out two months later, it might not have been acted on; Truman still hoped to curb defense spending. Still, NSC-68 commanded the support of virtually all high-ranking American officials . . . at the time it was delivered. It was music to the ears of the armed services. The Korean War then cinched the case for defense spending along the lines urged by the report. By fiscal 1952 the United States was paying $44 billion for national defense; by 1953, $50.4 billion, roughly the amount privately anticipated by advocates of NSC-68. Spending declined a little when the Korean War ended but still ranged between $40 and $53.5 billion every year between 1954 and 1964. Along with the decision for the Super, the logic of NSC-68 reflected the rapid militarization in American foreign policies following the Soviet atomic explosion and the "fall" of China.

Red Scare at Home

The toughening of American attitudes toward the Soviets in early 1950 did not exist in a cultural or political vacuum. On the contrary, events heated up already flammable anti-Communist emotions and ignited a Red Scare of considerable fire and fury. On January 21, ten days before Truman decided for the Super, a federal jury brought thirteen months of hotly contested litigation to a close by finding Alger Hiss, accused of having been a spy for the Soviets in the 1930s, guilty of perjury. Hiss, a middle-rank figure in foreign policy councils during the mid-1940s, was sentenced to five years in prison. On January 27 Klaus Fuchs, a German-born English atomic scientist who had worked on the A-bomb, was arrested for turning over secrets to the Soviets during and after the war. He was later tried in England, convicted, and imprisoned. On February 9 Senator Joseph McCarthy of Wisconsin alleged that Communists infested the American State Department. His accusations, offered to the Ohio County Women's Republican Club of Wheeling, West Virginia, increased pressure on the Truman administration to get tough with the Soviets. The Red Scare of "McCarthyism" helped to besmirch American politics and culture for much of the next five years.

The Superpowers Go to War in Korea

Arthur S. Link and William B. Catton

American fears of worldwide Communist domination were intensified in the summer of 1950 when Communist North Korea invaded democratic South Korea. Though American intervention, with UN support, turned back the invasion, Soviet and Chinese support of North Korea threatened to turn the civil war into a global conflict. Arthur S. Link and William B. Catton argue that the military stalemate in Korea had far-reaching consequences in America, particularly the rise in defense spending and in the number of federal agencies concerned with national security. Arthur S. Link, a professor of American history at Princeton University, is the recipient of Rockefeller, Guggenheim, and Rosenwald fellowships. William B. Catton is professor emeritus of history at Middlebury College.

[By] 1950, communism had become a major domestic political issue. Nothing disrupted the political peace more than the impact of developments in Asia on American public opinion. The Truman administration probably would have followed Great Britain, India, and other powers in recognizing the [Communist-led] People's Republic of China had Peking not launched a violent campaign in late 1949 to expel American diplomats, missionaries, and

Excerpted from "The Cold War Deepens," by Arthur S. Link and William B. Catton, in *American Epoch*, vol. 2, by Arthur S. Link, William A. Link, and William B. Catton (New York: Knopf, 1987). Reprinted with permission from The McGraw-Hill Companies.

private interests. Bitter anti-Peking sentiment in the United States was exacerbated by a so-called China lobby and by a Republican campaign to discredit the administration. . . .

The president, in January 1950, reaffirmed his determination not to be drawn into Chinese affairs. . . . And, a week later, Secretary of State Dean Acheson . . . announced what was in effect a new American policy in the Far East. The United States, he declared, would protect a "defensive perimeter" that ran from the Aleutians to Japan, . . . and the Philippines. But aggression against areas outside the perimeter—Korea, Taiwan, and Southeast Asia—would have to be met by the peoples involved and by the United Nations.

This speech gave new impetus to the Republican attack. It took an extreme turn as Senators Joseph McCarthy, Robert Taft, Kenneth S. Wherry of Nebraska, and other GOP spokesmen opened a campaign to drive Acheson from office and prove that the State Department was riddled with Communists and fellow travelers who, as Taft put it, had "surrendered to every demand of Russia . . . and promoted at every opportunity the Communist cause in China." This violent assault wrecked the previous bipartisan policy, made the formulation of a rational Far Eastern program impossible just when it was most needed, and raised grave doubts abroad about the quality of American leadership.

Other developments contributed to even greater soul searching. Truman's revelation in September 1949 that Russia had detonated a nuclear device upset the assumptions of American defensive strategy. It also renewed a fierce debate in administration circles . . . over the development of a hydrogen bomb, potentially a thousand times more powerful than the atomic bombs that had destroyed Hiroshima and Nagasaki. When Truman announced in January 1950 that he had ordered the AEC [Atomic Energy Commission] to proceed with work on the hydrogen bomb, thoughtful Americans were stunned by the gloomy prospects, even while agreeing that their government had no recourse. The American people were entering . . . a new era of "total diplomacy," in which their fortitude and wisdom would be put to severe and numerous tests.

Prelude to War

Not many months after Acheson spoke, an invasion of South Korea threatened world peace and sorely taxed American capacities. . . . Japan and Russia had fought a war for control of this strategic peninsula in 1904–1905, and Russian dominance there would gravely threaten Japanese security. Russian troops had entered northern Korea in August 1945; American forces had occupied southern Korea in September. The two powers agreed to divide their occupation zones at the thirty-eighth parallel, which runs north of the capital city of Seoul.

American leaders assumed that the Korean people would soon organize a government and that all occupation forces would thereupon be withdrawn. The Soviets in fact approved a plan in December 1945 to create a Korean government guided by a joint American-Soviet commission. But Russian representatives on the commission blocked all efforts at unification, established a Communist "people's government" in North Korea, and trained and equipped an army of 150,000 men. The United States then appealed to the UN General Assembly, which established a Temporary Commission on Korea in November 1947. It visited Seoul in January 1948 and, after being denied entry into the Soviet zone, held elections in South Korea. A constituent assembly met in July 1948, adopted a constitution, and elected Syngman Rhee as president. The UN, the United States, and other non-Communist powers recognized Rhee's regime as the only lawful government of Korea. Washington, following the advice of the Joint Chiefs of Staff and of General MacArthur in Japan, withdrew its last troops from South Korea in June 1949. It also gave substantial assistance to Rhee's government.

North Korea Invades the South

This, in general, was the situation when North Korean forces crossed the thirty-eighth parallel in an all-out inva-

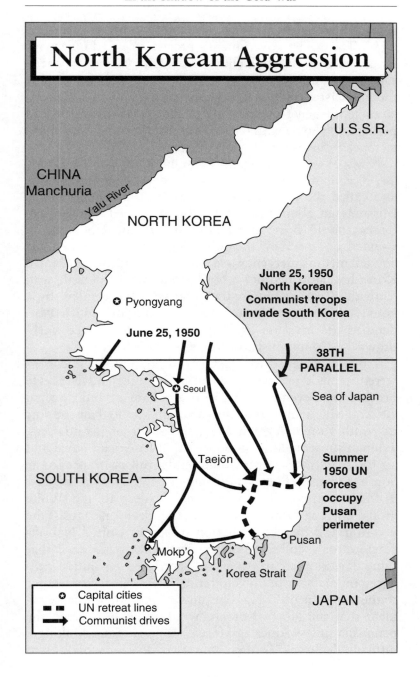

North Korean Aggression

U.S.S.R.

CHINA
Manchuria

Yalu River

NORTH KOREA

June 25, 1950
North Korean
Communist troops
invade South Korea

⊗ Pyongyang

June 25, 1950

38TH
PARALLEL

⊗ Seoul

Sea of Japan

Taejōn

SOUTH KOREA

Summer
1950 UN
forces
occupy
Pusan
perimeter

○ Pusan

Mokp'o

Korea Strait

JAPAN

⊗ Capital cities
▬ ▬ UN retreat lines
➔ Communist drives

sion of South Korea at 4 A.M., Korean time, on June 25, 1950. The Soviet government's precise role and objectives remain unclear. In all likelihood, the withdrawal of American troops and Acheson's statement that Korea lay outside the Far Eastern defense perimeter of the United States encouraged a belief on the part of the North Koreans, and perhaps the Soviets, that the United States would not fight to repel an invasion.

News of the war reached Washington at 9:26 P.M., June 24, Washington time. Acheson held hurried conferences and called the president (who was then in Independence, Missouri) at about midnight. Truman agreed that the secretary should bring the matter before the UN Security Council at once. By the following afternoon, when the council met in emergency session, it was evident that North Korea had launched not a border raid but a full-scale war. With the Russian representative absent, the council, by a vote of nine to zero, adopted a resolution which condemned the invasion as aggression and demanded withdrawal of Communist troops from South Korea.

Truman hastened to Washington on June 25 and conferred immediately with civilian and military advisers. He ordered the Seventh Fleet to protect Taiwan and directed General MacArthur to furnish arms and limited air support to South Korea. After hearing the views of his advisers, Truman subsequently announced that American naval and air forces in the Far East would render full assistance to the South Koreans. Events now moved swiftly to a climax. Truman summoned congressional leaders to the White House on June 27 and told them of his decision to resist the invasion and his determination to secure United Nations support for a collective effort. The Security Council that same day adopted an American-sponsored resolution calling upon member nations to render all necessary assistance to the Republic of Korea. On June 29 and 30, it became evident that the North Koreans would quickly overrun the peninsula unless American forces stopped them. Making a difficult decision, Truman sent two divisions of ground troops from Japan to South Korea and authorized a naval blockade of North Korea. This action was approved by the Joint Chiefs of Staff, the State Department, General MacArthur, and other advisers, all of whom assumed that American intervention would turn the tide and would not provoke Soviet or Chinese participation.

Truman's decision to intervene earned him, at least for the time being, widespread popular support. . . . Members of the House of Representatives stood and cheered when they learned that the president had ordered air and naval forces to defend South Korea. . . . Meanwhile, the Security Council established a UN command and requested the American government to name a commander in chief. Some nineteen nations soon made a military contribution, and by the end of 1950, British, Turkish, Australian, and Philippine troops were fighting alongside Americans and South Koreans, with General MacArthur in command.

The American Counterattack

Meanwhile, North Korean troops almost overran the entire peninsula before American power could be brought to bear. They had pressed the defenders into Korea's southeastern corner by September 12 and were threatening to drive them from Pusan, their remaining supply port. But UN defenses stiffened and held firm, and MacArthur counterattacked with large reinforcements on September 15, making a daring landing on the North Korean flank at Inchon. He soon recaptured Seoul, reoccupied southern Korea, and destroyed or captured more than half the invaders. UN forces had reached the thirty-eighth parallel by October 1 and were preparing to launch an invasion of North Korea.

Having cleared South Korea, victorious allied forces halted at the thirty-eighth parallel until the General Assembly of the United Nations, on October 7, 1950, called upon MacArthur to take all necessary steps to establish UN control throughout Korea. Although the Chinese foreign minister informed the Indian ambassador in Peking that "if

U.S. troops head toward the front during the Korean War. Despite initial success, North Korean forces were eventually pushed back to the Chinese border by a coordinated UN effort led by the United States.

the U.S. or U.N. forces crossed the Thirty-eighth Parallel, China would send troops to the Korean frontier to defend North Korea," few took the threat seriously. MacArthur assured Truman that there was little danger of Chinese intervention and promised a great slaughter if China's armies entered the fight.

MacArthur's forces drove triumphantly northward toward the Yalu River separating Korea from Manchuria. Just as it seemed that North Korean resistance had entirely collapsed, advanced American troops encountered large Chinese units fifty miles south of the Yalu in late October. Later reconnaissance revealed that China had massed armies of some 850,000 men in Manchuria and moved advanced units into northern Korea. While Chinese soldiers skirmished defensively, the Security Council heard Peking's representatives demand prompt American withdrawal from Korea.

MacArthur, on November 24, launched an offensive to drive the Chinese beyond the Yalu and end the war before Christmas. In this action he violated the spirit, if not the letter, of his instructions. It was the Washington government's policy to send only South Korean troops into this area in order to avoid provoking the Chinese. MacArthur's decision was also a nearly fatal strategic blunder, for he drove his men into a huge trap. The Chinese counterattacked on November 26 and split the center of the UN line, held by South Korean troops. The United States Eighth Army on the western flank withdrew in an orderly retreat toward the thirty-eighth parallel, but X [Tenth Army] Corps on the northeastern flank was isolated and cut off. It took the unit two weeks of desperate fighting to reach the port of Hungnam. From there, X Corps was evacuated and transferred to the main defensive line north of the thirty-eighth parallel, in one of modern warfare's most spectacular operations.

The Rise of the Military-Industrial Complex

In clear response to the heightened level of Soviet-American tension and to the perception of the need to contain Soviet expansionism, the Truman administration made a crucial decision to remobilize the United States. This historic change was clearly enunciated in an influential [National Security Council] document, NSC-68, written by Paul Nitze of the State Department. . . . Nitze . . . argued that the United States had to be prepared to respond to communism around the world. The Soviets, and world communism, were motivated by a "fanatic faith, antithetical to our own," which sought to "impose its absolute authority over the rest of the world." A proper American response . . . was preparation for long-term military and diplomatic competition with the Soviets. He proposed a wholesale militarization of peacetime society that would increase defense appropriations from an average of $15 billion to $30–$40 billion a year.

The outbreak of the Korean War inspired broad politi-

cal support for a program of remilitarization. . . . Congress
. . . approved plans to double the armed forces from 1.5
million to 3 million men by mid-1951. It adopted a rev-
enue bill designed to raise nearly $4.5 billion in additional
income and corporate taxes, and it appropriated another
$12.6 billion for defense and over $5 billion for military
assistance.

This increase in defense expenditures established a new
level which remained high even after the Korean armistice
in 1953. The militarization of American society and the
rise of a national security state that accompanied it brought
several clear consequences. It stimulated the growth of
what Eisenhower later called the "military-industrial complex" and committed the United States, historically a nation without large peacetime forces, to support a buildup

 ## Frozen Mountains, Freezing Men

*Korea was called "the war nobody wanted" because the country
was of little strategic value to the United States and soldiers
fought under conditions of harsh, desolate terrain and extreme
temperatures. War correspondent N. Harry Smith describes a typical December afternoon between battles in Korea in 1950.*

Inch by inch and yard by yard we progressed, the vehicles traveling about five miles an hour. The drivers sat hunched over the
steering wheels trying to negotiate the blind turns and the razor-
sharp, snow-covered rocks that protruded in clusters like so
many daggers. Tears of strain rolled out of their eyes and
dropped at their feet in tiny crystals of ice.

In the distance to the right, the mountains rose in jagged
peaks, the tempest of the howling wind swirled the snow across
the open canyon and spent its force upon the moving column.
Nothing froze but the already frozen; nothing remained in this
area but frozen mountains, freezing marching men, and sputter-

of both nuclear and conventional forces. It also spawned an array of new executive agencies, the most important of which was the National Security Agency. Their primary duty was to wage the cold war, through diplomatic, military, and sometimes covert means. . . .

It would be perhaps easy for the historian to conclude that Americans made this transition from isolation to global involvement calmly and wisely. The truth is, however, that the people nearly lost their heads [and] the Truman administration nearly lost control of foreign policy. . . .

Stalemate

The American Eighth Army halted the enemy drive in Korea and began a limited offensive in January 1951. With the UN presence in Korea secure, Truman and the Joint Chiefs

---

ing, steaming vehicles.

Water became an acute problem. Canteens were frozen solid, their plastic caps shattering into dozens of pieces. Food was out of the question. Rations were solid chunks of ice. Men hungered, thirsted, and froze. But the train always moved southward, closer to the bottom of the pass and the flat country below.

I thought to myself, Thank the good Lord for this opportunity to walk upon my frozen legs. I didn't want to ride in *any* vehicle over this hellish road, down a mountain that never leveled off into flatness. I didn't want to be seated in the jeep, holding on to it in prayer, praying every second that we would not run over a small stone in the road, slip, and be catapulted into the ravenous emptiness.

Men were shouting abuse upon the enemy and the elements as they trudged along. "The sonovabitch is bleedin'," spoke the man in front of me. The wind had cut his bearded face to ribbons.

N. Harry Smith, *The Korean War: Pusan to Chosin.* New York: Harcourt Brace Jovanovich, 1985.

quickly agreed upon a policy of conducting a limited war designed to maintain the integrity of South Korea, but one which would avert the danger of a general war with China—"the wrong war, at the wrong place, at the wrong time, and with the wrong enemy," as General Omar N. Bradley, chairman of the Joint Chiefs of Staff, later called it. . . .

MacArthur, however, was temperamentally incapable of accepting the concept of a limited war. . . . He therefore resorted to extreme measures. Informed on March 20, 1951, that the president was about to attempt to settle the Korean conflict by diplomacy, MacArthur issued a public statement calculated to prevent a peaceful settlement. . . . "We must win," he concluded. "There is no substitute for victory.". . .

Meanwhile, on several fronts, the Americans had moved to convince the North Koreans and Chinese that a settlement would be to their advantage. . . . In Korea, UN forces repulsed two major offensives in April and May 1951 with staggering losses to the attackers. By midyear, it appeared that American policy was succeeding. The Communists had suffered over a million casualties; the best Chinese armies had been decimated; and China was isolated diplomatically and economically from the non-Communist world and had no hope of forcing a military decision. . . .

When it became clear to both sides that a military victory was not possible, truce negotiations began in July 1951. The Chinese and Koreans in November 1951 dropped their demand for UN withdrawal southward to the thirty-eighth parallel and accepted the American demand for demarcation along the military line at the time an armistice was signed. But, in October 1952, these negotiations were broken off after the Communists demanded the forcible delivery of some 46,000 Chinese and North Koreans who did not wish to go home. Only after the inauguration of the new Eisenhower administration was the impasse ended. Eisenhower and [John Foster Dulles, adviser to the State Department] were determined to use nuclear weapons to resolve the stalemate, and the Chinese knew this fact. Rather than face nuclear weapons, the Chinese and South Koreans yielded, and an armistice was signed at Panmunjom on July 27, 1953. It ended the Korean War, a military conflict that had cost the United States 54,246 dead, 103,284 wounded, and billions of dollars.

Building the Hydrogen Bomb

Robert J. Donovan

By 1950 the Soviet Union had exploded an atom bomb, ending America's four-year monopoly on the weapon. Fear of nuclear war with the Soviets drove U.S. generals and some politicians to spend billions of tax dollars to develop the next generation of nuclear weapons, the "super" or hydrogen bomb. Robert J. Donovan, a White House correspondent during the Truman years, traces the development process in the following article.

By the start of 1950 the time was approaching for Truman to decide whether to initiate a program to build a hydrogen bomb. In the previous October he had approved a major acceleration in the production of atomic bombs. Even before "Operation Joe," the American code name for the Soviet atomic explosion in September, the military had been seeking a larger stockpile of American atomic bombs. The Soviet success had made that seem more urgent than ever not only to the military but also to the president's civilian advisers, and pressure for a reassuring response to the Soviet bomb was rising in Congress through the powerful Joint Committee on Atomic Energy.

While Truman was still deliberating the expansion of atomic bomb production, [Atomic Energy Commissioner] Lewis Strauss made his proposal to fellow members of the . . . commission to meet the new Soviet challenge with a

Excerpted from *Tumultuous Years*, by Robert J. Donovan (New York: Norton, 1982). Copyright ©1982 by Robert J. Donovan. Reprinted with permission from Sterling Lord Literistic, Inc.

crash program to manufacture a hydrogen bomb. . . . Strauss had his proposal brought to Truman's attention in October 1949. According to Richard G. Hewlett and Francis Duncan, official historians of the Atomic Energy Commission, Truman apparently had never heard of the theoretical hydrogen bomb but showed an immediate interest, which was not surprising in a president at a time when Congress and the country demanded action in the wake of the Soviet blast. The public, of course, knew nothing of any of this, Strauss's proposal having been made in the secrecy of the Atomic Energy Commission.

Dr. Wendell M. Latimer, dean of the department of chemistry at the University of California at Berkeley, was worried about the possibility that the Soviets might move directly into development of a hydrogen bomb as a means of offsetting America's lead in atomic bombs. He mentioned his concern to Dr. Ernest O. Lawrence, winner of the Nobel Prize in physics, one of the developers of the atomic bomb, and then director of the Atomic Energy Commission's radiation laboratory at Berkeley. In turn Lawrence discussed Latimer's concern with a scientific colleague there, Dr. Luis W. Alvarez. Together they agreed, according to Hewlett and Duncan, that a hydrogen bomb "would be an effective response to the Soviet threat." Scheduled to go to Washington in any case, Lawrence decided to take Alvarez with him to stir up interest for such a bomb. On the way, the two stopped at the Los Alamos Scientific Laboratory in New Mexico to consult Dr. Edward Teller, an early advocate of building the atomic bomb and a believer in the feasibility of a thermonuclear weapon, whose principal developer he was to be.

Encouraged by Teller, Lawrence and Alvarez arrived in Washington on October 8, 1949, and talked with the Atomic Energy Commission staff and lunched with McMahon, the chairman, and another member of the Joint Congressional Committee on Atomic Energy. "The outcome," reported Hewlett and Duncan, "was predictable: The legislators and the scientists were more than ever convinced that the superweapon might well save the nation from the Soviet threat." McMahon dispatched a subcommittee to Los Alamos and Berkeley to explore the prospects of a hydrogen bomb. . . .

[Nuclear physicist Robert J. Oppenheimer wrote: "Meanwhile a] joint congressional committee, having tried to find something tangible to chew on ever since [Operation Joe], has at least found its answer. We must have a super, and we must have it fast. . . . The joint chiefs appear informally to have decided to give the development . . . overriding priority. . . . The climate of opinion among the competent physicists also shows signs of shifting."

Debating the Moral Costs

Pinpointing a situation that was certain to bring great pressure on Truman, [nuclear physicist Robert] Oppenheimer concluded: "What does worry me is that this thing appears to have caught the imagination, both of the congressional and of military people, as the answer to the problem posed by the Russian advance. It would be folly to oppose the exploration of this weapon. We have always known it had to be done; and it does have to be done.". . .

The general advisory committee [of nuclear scientists] met without public notice and on October 30, 1949, unanimously recommended against a crash program to build a hydrogen bomb—a weapon, they said, whose energy release would be from one hundred to one thousand times greater and whose destructive power in terms of area damage would be from twenty to one hundred times greater than those of the existing atomic bombs. The members objected on both technical and moral grounds.

As to the former, they held that construction of a hydrogen bomb probably would require large amounts of tritium, necessitating immense reactor capacity. Research on such a weapon was in so early a stage that theoretical design studies had not yet been completed or tested.

On the moral side, a statement signed by six members . . . held that "the extreme dangers to mankind inherent in the proposal outweigh any military advantage that could come from this development." Two other members—Dr. Enrico Fermi of the University of Chicago Institute for Nuclear Studies and Dr. Isidor I. Rabi of Columbia University, a Nobel laureate in physics—appended an opinion. They asserted that a hydrogen bomb would go "far beyond any military objective and [enter] the range of very great natural catastrophes. By its very nature it cannot be confined to a military objective but becomes a weapon which in practical effect is almost one of genocide."

The statement of the six members, written by [Harvard president James Bryant] Conant, noted that a hydrogen bomb would be "in a totally different category from an atomic bomb," because of the vast range of destruction. "Its use," the statement said, "would involve a decision to slaughter a vast number of civilians. . . . Therefore, a superbomb might become a weapon of genocide.". . .

[Fermi and Rabi] suggested that instead of building a hydrogen bomb, the United States "invite the nations of the world to join us in a solemn pledge not to proceed in the development or construction of weapons in this category." What was to be done in the event that the Soviet Union refused to make such a pledge the scientists did not say.

These statements were classified top secret and remained unknown to the public for many years. . . .

"Technically Sweet"

Along with the pressures, there was developing behind the hydrogen bomb proposal a momentum similar to that which had carried along the atomic bomb program. Scientists were aroused by the challenge of mastering a hydrogen bomb. As Oppenheimer was to testify in 1954 in connection with the decision to build it, "when you see something that is technically sweet, you go ahead and do it and you argue about what to do about it only after you have had your technical success. That is the way it was with the atomic bomb. I do not think anybody opposed making it: there were some debates about what to do with it after it was made." "If there is a new possibility," [physicist Edward] Teller said afterward, regarding the hydrogen bomb, "I would like to see it explored and developed. . . . I did believe in science and in progress and in finding out

Truman's Thoughts on Nuclear War

In 1957, five years after he left office, Harry Truman told a television interviewer that he had no regrets about dropping atom bombs on Hiroshima and Nagasaki to end World War II. His comments drew a letter of protest from the city council of Hiroshima calling for the former president to decry the future use of nuclear weapons under any circumstances. Truman penned a letter, found undelivered many years later, in which he called for an international police force that would prevent small battles from turning into all-out nuclear war.

The world is faced with a situation that means either total destruction or the greatest age in history can be its lot.

The decision must be made and it must be made as soon as possible. The great nations and the great peoples of the earth have all been through trials and great difficulties down through the ages. They have fought each other for sovereignty and control along with the exploitation of their resources. All that has been accomplished is a return to old concepts and old ideas.

Down through the ages there have been men whose concept of life was to live creditably and to help others to live happily. The Chinese, the East Indians, the Arabians, the Jews and the comparatively modern-day Christians have produced ideas and moral codes for the ideal of men's living together in harmony.

Usually these great ideas have been exploited by selfish rulers and debauched priesthoods for power and control at the expense of the very people whom the great idealists wanted to help.

Now we are faced with total destruction. The old Hebrew Prophets presented the idea of the destruction of the world by

what can be done. And I did have the confidence that there was at least a good possibility what we developed would be properly used rather than misused."

Because of the magnitude of the decision before him, Tru-

fire after their presentation of a destruction by water.

Well, that destruction is at hand unless the great leaders of the world prevent it.

Two thousand American scientists have presented an "Appeal to the Governments and Peoples of the World" to the President of the United States.

Eleven thousand scientists from forty-nine nations have presented to the Secretary General of the United Nations in this year of 1958 a story of their spontaneous concern over the nuclear threat to humanity.

Those of the world who still believe in morality and justice are in the vast majority. That is true not only in the free nations but it is true in Russia, in China, in Spain, in Portugal, in the Near East, in South America, where the dictators preside.

The leader of one of the great nations whose voice can be heard and listened to should go to the Assembly of the United Nations and advocate an international control of nuclear energy in the interest of all mankind. He should advocate an international police force for the enforcement of control and the maintenance of peace in the Near East, the Far East, the Pacific, the Atlantic, and all around the world. No little dictator anywhere should be permitted to oppress his own people or to use the methods of a demagogue to upset the peace of the world and bring about its complete destruction.

These rules to apply to the big dictators and to all nations free or slave, all around the world—and then maybe destruction by fire will not come about.

It is up to our leaders.

Robert H. Ferrell, ed., *Harry S. Truman and the Bomb*. Worland, WY: High Plains, 1996.

man on November 19 revived the special committee of the National Security Council . . . which he had appointed in 1949 to advise him on the atomic energy program. He directed that the committee secretly analyze the technical, military, and political aspects of the hydrogen bomb question and submit a recommendation to him. The outcome was hardly in doubt. On the basis of their known attitudes [members of the committee] were almost certain to favor moving ahead on a hydrogen bomb program. [A member of the committee, David] Lilienthal later observed, "Our policy was to get rid of atomic bombs through international control on the one hand, and yet our military was relying on these weapons as virtually our only means of defense.". . .

By [this time] the newspapers were playing up speculation about the superbomb and whether it would be approved by the president. Within the special committee differences had arisen, and these were rumored in the press. Lilienthal maintained that a decision to proceed with the bomb might close the door to international control. . . .

On January 27 [1950] Dr. Harold C. Urey of the University of Chicago, a Nobel laureate and one of the developers of the atomic bomb, said in a speech: "The hydrogen bomb should be . . . built. I do not think we should intentionally lose the armaments race; to do this will be to lose our liberties.". . .

[On January 31] Truman . . . indicated to his staff that he had made up his mind. He did not disclose his decision then. . . . The basic recommendation agreed upon . . . was that the president approve a program to determine the technical feasibility of a thermonuclear weapon. . . . At the same time the committee, significantly, recommended that Truman direct the secretaries of state and defense "to undertake a reexamination of our objectives in peace and war and of the effect of these objectives on our strategic plans, in light of the probable fission [atomic] bomb capability and possible thermonuclear bomb capability of the Soviet Union.". . .

The White House issued a public statement that same January 31, declaring, laconically, that the president had ordered the Atomic Energy Commission "to continue its work on all forms of atomic weapons, including the so-called hydrogen or superbomb." Public and congressional approval was overwhelming. A *Washington Post* editorial said: "The bomb will be constructed because we dare not afford not to build it. It would be a shirking of responsibility to leave the American people one fine day to face a stand-and-deliver ultimatum from a Soviet Union armed with an H-bomb."

In forty-eight hours Truman's compromise solution simply to "investigate the feasibility" of a hydrogen bomb was blown to pieces. On February 2 Dr. Klaus Emil Julius Fuchs, chief of the theoretical physics division of the British Atomic Energy Research Establishment, who had worked on the American atomic bomb, was arrested in London, charged with engaging in nuclear espionage for the Soviet Union. The news undercut those who had argued that the United States should seek a control agreement with Moscow before building a hydrogen bomb. Only by creating strategic areas of strength around the world could the allied powers stop the expansion of communism, Acheson told a press conference. The Joint Chiefs of Staff took a new look at the situation. "They are of the opinion, with which I fully concur," [Secretary of Defense] Louis Johnson wrote to Truman, "that it is incumbent upon the United States to proceed forthwith on an all-out program of hydrogen-bomb development. . . ." Around November 1, 1949, the Soviets had begun actual work on a thermonuclear bomb. Truman accepted the advice of his advisers and on March 10, 1950, approved an urgent program to build a hydrogen bomb. At the critical juncture in the winter of 1949–50, neither the United States nor the Soviet Union approached the other to discuss banning thermonuclear weapons.

A Soviet View of the Cold War

Vladislav Zubok and Constantine Pleshakov

Modern analysts of the cold war era question whether the United States overestimated and overreacted to the Communist threat. Since the end of the cold war, however, many declassified Soviet documents prove that the USSR intentionally triggered confrontations in Korea and elsewhere in an attempt to manipulate U.S. leaders and their policies. The results were a nuclear arms race and anti-Communist hysteria in the United States.

As two Soviet citizens who grew up in Russia during the cold war, Vladislav Zubok and Constantine Pleshakov offer a unique perspective of Soviet ambitions. Zubok is a senior fellow at the National Security Archive in Washington, D.C., and Pleshakov is the director of the Pacific Studies Center at the Institute of U.S. and Canada Studies in Moscow.

S talin in 1945 was second only to Hitler as modern history's greatest murderer and ruler, if greatness is measured in the destruction of human lives and the number of territories conquered. His achievements could be matched only by his failures. In just a few years he decimated the Russian peasantry and built on its bones Europe's biggest war machine, rivaling that of Nazi Germany. He then viciously destroyed the commanding core of his army, interfered with the development and production of war technologies, and

Excerpted by permission of the publisher from *Inside the Kremlin's Cold War: From Stalin to Khrushchev,* by Vladislav Zubok and Constantine Pleshakov (Cambridge, MA: Harvard University Press). Copyright ©1996 by the President and Fellows of Harvard College.

massacred, in a frenzy of political and social "cleansing," millions of loyal supporters, skillful professionals and workers. He divided Eastern Europe with Hitler, annexing a large part of it with its millions of inhabitants. Then he got bogged down ignominiously in a war with tiny Finland, and let himself be taken by surprise by Hitler's armies. During the first months of World War II he lost three million soldiers and officers, as well as the most industrially and agriculturally significant territories of the country.

The Nazis were driven back from Moscow in December 1941, but in the next year Stalin's autocratic whims triggered another military catastrophe that brought the Wehrmacht to the river Volga and the Caucasus. In 1943–1945 the Soviet army turned back the tide, pushed the nine million German troops and Germany's satellite armies back to Berlin, and occupied most of Central and Eastern Europe. In Manchuria the Soviet army, together with the United States, thoroughly defeated a historic rival of Russia in the Far East—imperial Japan. Now the Soviet Union dominated Eurasia just as imperial Russia had after Napoleon's defeat in 1815. The price of these victories was twenty-seven million Soviet lives—a loss from which the Soviet Union would never fully recover. . . .

On March 5, 1953, Stalin, paralyzed by a stroke, died in his dacha near Moscow. Less than six months later, on August 12, the USSR tested the world's first deliverable hydrogen bomb, equivalent to 400,000 TNT. Together, the death of the universal Communist leader and the appearance of this weapon of global destruction constituted, perhaps, the most far-reaching event in the course of the early Cold War.

The Soviet H-Bomb

The steps taken by both the Soviet Union and the United States toward producing the "super-weapon" on a massive scale (the United States had tested the first thermonuclear device in November 1952) led to the possibility that any conflict between the two could result not only in another devastating world war but in the destruction of the human race. This new reality would have been a severe test for the foreign policy of any state. For Soviet foreign policy, locked into the revolutionary-imperial paradigm in the last years of Stalin's rule, it represented a seemingly impossible challenge.

The death of Stalin shattered the foundations of Soviet domestic and foreign policy. The Soviet empire, personified by one man, was in serious danger. Its fate very much depended on who would pick up the fallen scepter of the universal Communist cause and what means would be used for its preservation and strengthening. . . .

"We Must Be Prepared"

On February 4, 1954, the Party Secretariat (the body directly under [Stalin's successor Nikita] Khrushchev) sanctioned upgrading underground bunkers and bomb shelters for the military and government. The resulting subterranean "city" spread hundreds of feet deep under party headquarters and the Kremlin, leading for miles away from downtown Moscow. It was expanded again in 1959.

Stalin, despite his interest in the Bomb, had never grasped the new meaning the Cold War acquired in the nuclear age. Khrushchev understood that nuclear bipolarity became the basic feature of the Cold War, as both the Soviet Union and the United States gained the capacity to destroy each other and the whole world. In May 1957 Khrushchev, interviewed by the *New York Times*, said that "the international tension [the Cold War] apparently boils down in the final analysis to the relations between two countries—the Soviet Union and the United States of America." Khrushchev, for all his later bravado, developed a sense of the ultimate limits imposed by nuclear weapons on statesmanship. . . .

Yet the philosophy of prudence and caution went against Khrushchev's grain. As with many optimists, his energy and imagination could not be paralyzed by fear of nuclear war. As he recalled, his nuclear credo since 1953 had been that "we could never possibly use these [nuclear] weapons, but all the same we must be prepared. Our understanding is not a sufficient answer to the arrogance of the imperialists.". . .

Khrushchev's revolutionary side could not help rejoicing at the thought that, with the advent of nuclear deadlock and missile technology, the end of American arrogance and superiority was within sight. The Geneva summit with Dwight Eisenhower greatly influenced Khrushchev's thinking about nuclear deterrence. He understood, in his own words, that "there was not any sort of pre-war situation," and that Americans "feared us as much as we feared them.". . .

The Soviet leader quickly understood that the nuclear sword cut both ways: the Americans used it to contain communism and, if possible, roll it back. Why shouldn't the Soviets similarly use it to contain American imperialism and, by providing an "atomic umbrella" for the anticolonialism movements, accelerate the roll-back of capitalism?

The CIA in Guatemala

John Ranelagh

In December 1947, President Truman signed the National Security Act, creating several top-secret government agencies, including the Central Intelligence Agency (CIA). The official mission of the CIA was to gather information about Soviet movements in foreign countries, but its scope was broadened considerably to include direct intervention in the politics and economies of sovereign nations.

The CIA's mandate was to employ methods ranging from propaganda, economic sabotage, and subversion to paramilitary operations against any government deemed a threat to U.S. interests, whether an enemy, such as Communist East Germany, or an ally, such as Italy.

Legislation approved in 1949 authorized the CIA to spend money without congressional oversight. When socialist-leaning Jacobo Arbenz was democratically elected president of the Central American country of Guatemala in 1951, the CIA used its broad powers to overthrow the Arbenz government. Although the operation was considered a success at the time, it permanently destabilized Guatemala. Over the next forty years various factions would fight for control of the country and more than one hundred thousand people would die.

John Ranelagh describes U.S. involvement in Guatemala in this selection. Ranelagh is a British television producer and the author of two books on the history of Ireland.

Excerpted from *The Agency: The Rise and Decline of the CIA*, by John Ranelagh. Copyright ©1986 by Cambridge Publishing, Ltd. Reprinted with permission from Simon & Schuster, Inc.

[A ccording to senior operations officer Tom Braden, the CIA] never had to account for the money it spent except to the President if the President wanted to know how much money it was spending. But otherwise the funds were not only unaccountable, they were unvouchered, so there was really no means of checking them—"unvouchered funds" meaning expenditures that don't have to be accounted for. . . . If the director of the CIA wanted to extend a present, say, to someone in Europe—a Labour leader— suppose he just thought, This man can use fifty thousand dollars, he's working well and doing a good job—he could hand it to him and never have to account to anybody. . . . I don't mean to imply that there were a great many of them that were handed out as Christmas presents. They were handed out for work well performed or in order to perform work well. . . . Politicians in Europe, particularly right after the war, got a lot of money from the CIA. . . .

Since it was unaccountable, it could hire as many people as it wanted. It never had to say to any committee—no committee said to it—"You can only have so many men." It could do exactly as it pleased. It made preparations therefore for every contingency. It could hire armies; it could buy banks. There was simply no limit to the money it could spend and no limit to the people it could hire and no limit to the activities it could decide were necessary to conduct the war—the secret war. . . . It was a multinational. Maybe it was one of the first. . . .

Seizing United Fruit Company Lands

[The CIA decided to use this covert power to overthrow Guatemalan president Jacobo Arbenz.] Arbenz, who had come to power as the country's second democratically elected president in March 1951, found that his political base depended on continuing the social and economic reform [already underway in Guatemala. He was backed] by the militancy of the small but important Communist party and the large, effective labor groupings that supported Arbenz and on whose votes he relied.

The situation brought about a polarization in Guatemalan politics between Arbenz on one side and the strong, agrarian, commercial, conservative opposition on the other. In 1953 Arbenz confiscated the United Fruit Company's holdings. [Secretary of State] John Foster Dulles heeded the company's complaints and pressed Arbenz for compensation. Arbenz refused, largely because the country could not afford to pay proper compensation. . . . This cleared the way for action. On the diplomatic front, the State Department secured a condemnation of Guatemala's actions from the Tenth Inter-American Conference meeting in March 1954. Secretly, plans that had been made by the CIA in 1952 to overthrow Arbenz by supporting Guatemalan exiles and mercenaries in Nicaragua were dusted off and expanded. Colonel J.C. King, chief of the Western Hemisphere division in the CIA's Directorate of Plans, was put in charge. . . . King had more faith in military approaches to covert operations than in sophisticated political ones. He put the CIA into action by organizing a "revolt" in the town of Salamá, provincial capital not far from Guatemala City. Two hundred guerrillas held the town for seventeen hours before being arrested after a brief gunfight in which four of the guerrillas were killed. King was pulled off the operation, and Frank Wisner was given direct charge.

Wisner took stock of the project and determined to demonstrate the way in which [CIA founder "Wild Bill"] Donovan's ideas of first softening up a target with sabotage, propaganda, and commando raids and then following through with a thoroughgoing attack could be used in peacetime. He named the project Operation Success. . . .

Using a Secret Air Force

Between January and mid-June 1954 the CIA spent, by some estimates, about $20 million, organizing a guerrilla army and a secret air force, setting up secret radio stations, and finding a leader—Colonel Carlos Castillo Armas—to replace Arbenz. On May 15 the CIA was able to confirm that a Swedish freighter, the *Alfhem*, had delivered 15,424 cases of Czech military supplies at Puerto Barrios, Guatemala's east-coast port.

This news shook Washington and removed any remaining restraints on Operation Success. With air support, Armas launched an attack on Guatemala City on June 18 and within days overthrew Arbenz. In Washington everyone was delighted. John Foster Dulles hailed the Armas government in glowing terms, and President Eisenhower asked the CIA for another personal briefing. . . .

The nature of Arbenz's government, however, meant that Operation Success launched both the CIA and the United States on a new path. . . . Arbenz . . . had simply been trying to reform his country and had not sought foreign help in this. Thus by overthrowing him, America was in effect making a new decision in the cold war. . . . Now internal subversion—communism from within—was cause for direct action. What was not said . . . was that the exercise of American power, even clandestinely through the CIA, would not be undertaken where Soviet power was already established. In addition, regardless of the principles being professed, when direct action was taken (whether clandestine or not), the interests of American business would be a consideration: if the flag was to follow, it would quite definitely follow trade. . . .

After World War II, American governments were more willing to use their influence and strength all over the world for the first time and to see an ideological implication in the "persecution" of U.S. business interests.

CHAPTER 2

The Cold War at Home

AMERICA'S DECADES

The Rosenberg Spy Case

Ronald Radosh and Joyce Milton

Ronald Radosh and Joyce Milton provide historical background to the Rosenberg case in this selection. The Soviet Union exploded its first atom bomb in 1949. Many in the United States were skeptical that Soviet scientists had developed the bomb on their own, and some believed that spies must have given the Soviets atomic secrets. When German-born physicist Klaus Fuchs, arrested in England, confessed to giving the Soviets top-secret information when he was working on the American A-bomb in the United States in 1946, he implicated others who in turn named Julius Rosenberg, an American electrical engineer in New York City.

Rosenberg and his wife, Ethel, were arrested, convicted, and executed in the electric chair at the infamous Sing Sing prison in New York. The case generated worldwide publicity and an outcry for clemency for the couple, who left two young sons. Many believed the government framed the couple, or at least Ethel, who was arrested to put pressure on Julius to confess, which he never did. After the collapse of the Soviet Union in 1990, however, documents came to light showing that the Rosenbergs did have contacts with Soviet agents. The full extent of their involvement is still unknown.

Ronald Radosh is a professor of history at Queensborough and at the Graduate Center of the City University of

Excerpted from *The Rosenberg File: A Search for the Truth,* by Ronald Radosh and Joyce Milton (New York: Holt, Rinehart, and Winston, 1983). Copyright ©1983 by Ronald Radosh and Joyce Milton. Reprinted with permission from International Creative Management, Inc.

New York. Joyce Milton is a nationally recognized reporter and critic whose work has appeared in dozens of national magazines.

B y the summer of 1950, Julius and Ethel Rosenberg were to all appearances a quite unremarkable young married couple. They were the parents of two sons—Michael, born in 1943, and Robert, born in 1947—and they lived in a three-room apartment in a modern high-rise development located in the same neighborhood where they had both been born and reared. Neither Julius nor Ethel had been politically active for some years. Nor is there any indication that the Rosenbergs' names had come to the attention of any government investigative body since Julius's dismissal by the [Army] Signal Corps five years earlier [for allegedly joining the Communist Party]. The Rosenbergs could be said to be unusual only to the extent that business troubles and Ethel's bouts of ill health had kept them from enjoying the prosperity that came to so many of their peers after the war.

But the Rosenbergs' lives were changed forever on the night of June 15, 1950, when David Greenglass, Ethel's brother, named Julius Rosenberg as the man who had recruited him to spy for the Soviet Union. Julius Rosenberg was arrested one month later on a charge of conspiracy to commit espionage, and Ethel was arraigned on the same charge on August 11. At their trial the following March, David Greenglass, backed up by his wife, Ruth, claimed that Julius had begun spying for the Russians while still employed by the Signal Corps and by 1945 had been in a position to deliver atomic secrets provided by Greenglass directly to Soviet agents. After the war, moreover, he had been a master spy controlling a network that included contacts in upstate New York and Ohio. The Greenglasses also claimed that Ethel Rosenberg had known and approved of her husband's activities, and that on one occasion she had assisted her husband by typing David's handwritten notes containing a description of the atomic bomb.

Maintaining Their Innocence

The Rosenbergs' response to these accusations was to call them a malicious invention: the Greenglasses knew that they could win leniency for their own crimes, whatever

Despite their declarations of innocence, Ethel and Julius Rosenberg were convicted of espionage.

they may have been, by pointing their fingers at supposedly more important traitors. Julius and Ethel were vulnerable because of their past political associations, and it was all too easy for David and Ruth to name their in-laws, settling their grudge over the failure of the family business in the bargain. The Rosenbergs continued to proclaim their innocence, both during their trial and throughout more than two years spent on death row awaiting execution, with a tenacity that impressed many who had originally believed them guilty.

The contrast between the fanatical, veteran spies described by the Greenglasses and the victimized law-abiding couple that the Rosenbergs claimed to be could not have been more striking. But, wherever the truth lay, something more than a family feud run out of control had to be involved. If the Rosenbergs were framed, this could hardly have been accomplished without the knowing participation of key figures in the Federal Bureau of Investigation and on the federal prosecutor's staff. On the other hand, if the Greenglasses' charges were true, then one must ask how the Rosenberg spy network could have operated undetected for more than five years. And why, even after David Greenglass's confession, was the government able to bring charges against only one other alleged member of the ring—a thirty-three-year-old electrical engineer named Morton Sobell?

The judge who sentenced Julius and Ethel Rosenberg to death called their crime "worse than murder," charging them with the responsibility for the Korean conflict and for the millions who might yet die in a Soviet atomic attack. The Rosenbergs' position, expressed in scores of letters written from their cells in Sing Sing penitentiary, was that they were innocent victims of capitalist justice. . . . The reality that lay behind these two rhetorical extremes is the hidden Rosenberg case.

The Cold War and McCarthyism

Douglas T. Miller and Marion Nowak

Douglas T. Miller and Marion Nowak present a historical overview of the cold war in this selection. The Soviet Union and the United States were uneasy allies in World War II, and Soviet participation was instrumental in defeating the Nazis. But before the war, Soviet dictator Joseph Stalin had murdered up to 30 million of his fellow Soviet citizens through deliberate starvation, execution, and forced labor. After the war, Stalin imposed strict Communist authority over the nations of Eastern Europe, alarming and angering the United States and other democracies throughout the world.

In the United States, the fear of worldwide Soviet domination led to drastic measures taken against thousands of Americans whose sympathies with Russian revolutionary politics during the 1930s depression were held up as subversive after the war. In the anti-Communist hysteria that swept America, thousands were forced to take loyalty oaths and pressured to name friends and relatives believed to be Communist sympathizers. The witchhunt was led by Wisconsin senator Joseph McCarthy, who charged, usually without proof, that tens of thousands of Communists had infiltrated the U.S. government, academia, the arts, and the media.

Douglas T. Miller is an associate professor of history at the University of Michigan. Marion Nowak is a journalist who has lectured at Michigan State.

Excerpted from *The Fifties: The Way We Really Were*, by Douglas T. Miller and Marion Nowak. Copyright ©1975, 1977 by Douglas T. Miller and Marion Nowak. Reprinted with permission from Douglas T. Miller.

The wartime alliance of convenience between the United States and the Soviet Union temporarily subdued [anti-Communist feelings in the U.S.]. But soon after World War II, as relations between the two superpowers rapidly deteriorated, fears of an internal communist threat reemerged with renewed vehemence. More than ever right-wing propaganda equated all liberalism with the Red menace. In the 1946 congressional elections, Republicans, making frequent use of that equation, gained a majority for the first time in 18 years. . . .

The immediate postwar years were frustrating times. Domestically, people suffered from inflation, unemployment, strikes, racial tensions, fear of renewed depression, and the general dislocations caused by the rapid attempt to adjust from war to peace. International affairs were also extremely worrisome as it quickly became clear that the great sacrifices of the war years had not brought instant tranquillity.

In March 1947, President Harry S Truman, genuinely concerned about . . . Soviet aggressions and seeking to head off Republican attacks on the patriotism of Democrats, committed the United States to a policy aimed at defeating communism abroad and at home. On March 12, 1947, he announced what became known as the Truman Doctrine: "It must be the policy of the United States to support free peoples who are resisting attempted subjugation by armed minorities." This policy pledged the nation to the cold war—a reliance on maintaining military superiority in a world pictured as irreconcilably divided into camps of good and evil. Less than two weeks later, on March 22, the President launched his domestic war against communism. Truman issued Executive Order 9835 initiating a loyalty review program with the stated purpose of effecting "maximum protection" to "the United States against infiltration of disloyal persons into the ranks of its employees."

Though Truman would later complain of the "great wave of hysteria" sweeping the nation, his commitment to victory over communism, to completely safeguarding the

United States from external and internal threats, was in large measure responsible for creating that very hysteria. Between the launching of his security program in March 1947 and December 1952, some 6.6 million persons were investigated. Not a single case of espionage was uncovered, though about 500 persons were dismissed in dubious cases of "questionable loyalty." All of this was conducted with secret evidence, secret and often paid informers, and neither judge nor jury. Despite the failure to find subversion, the broad scope of the official Red hunt gave popular credence to the notion that the government was riddled with spies. A conservative and fearful reaction coursed the country. Americans became convinced of the need for absolute security and the preservation of the established order.

Not to be outdone by the federal government, states, cities, and counties set up their own loyalty programs. So too did many corporations, educational institutions, and labor unions. Publicly pledging allegiance to God, country, and constitution, while abjuring communist affiliations, became a basic feature of American life. Under the guise of loyalty checks, conservatives ferreted out not communists but liberals, New Dealers, radical labor leaders, civil rights activists, pacifists, atheists.

Communism Abroad, Spies at Home

From the time of Truman's 1947 executive order through the early fifties, a series of external events contributed to the growing internal anticommunist mania. In 1948 a communist coup succeeded in Czechoslovakia and the Soviets blocked Allied ground entry into Berlin. Nineteen forty-nine was more shocking as China, which Americans had always regarded as practically their own, became communist. To make matters worse, the Soviets exploded their first nuclear weapon, breaking the American monopoly. Then in June 1950 fighting broke out in distant Korea. For the next three years U.S. troops fought North Korean and Chinese communists to a frustrating stalemate in a war Americans were told was necessary to stop Soviet-sponsored aggression. . . .

While troubles abroad deeply disturbed Americans, domestic witch hunting in the late forties and early fifties had equally disquieting effects. On July 20, 1948, a federal grand jury indicted 11 leaders of the Communist party of the United States. They were charged with conspiracy to advocate the overthrow of the U.S. Government by force. The defendants were not proved to be agents of the Soviet Union; nor were they even charged with engaging in espionage. In a much publicized ten-month trial that began in January 1949, the prosecutors established that the communist leaders advocated the principles of Marxism-Leninism, which in the atmosphere of the time was enough to convict them.

On January 21, 1950, Alger Hiss was convicted of perjury following two of the most sensational and highly publicized trials in American history. The Hiss case first came to national attention in August 1948 when at an HUAC [House Un-American Activities Committee] hearing Whittaker Chambers, a confessed ex-communist, accused Hiss of having been a party member while employed in the State Department during the 1930s. Initially Chambers' charges were vague. But with prodding from [California representative Richard M.] Nixon and other committee members, he soon told a story of stolen documents passed from Hiss to himself to the Soviets. Though Hiss could not be tried for espionage due to the statute of limitations, a New York grand jury indicted him for perjury. A first trial ended in a hung jury. A second much publicized and still controversial trial resulted in Hiss' conviction. . . .

On February 3, 1950, only two weeks after Hiss' conviction, the British Government announced the arrest of Dr. Klaus Fuchs, a high-level atomic scientist who had worked at Los Alamos during the war. Fuchs confessed to having spied for the Soviet Union. Investigators linked him to Americans Harry Gold, Morton Sobell, and Julius and Ethel Rosenberg. All of these Americans were arrested, tried, and convicted of conspiracy to commit espionage. Gold and Sobell received long jail terms. The Rosenbergs were executed.

These events of 1949–50 shocked and stunned Americans. How could Russia have the Bomb? How could China have fallen to the communists? How many Alger Hisses must there still be in government?

"Reds Are After Your Child"

The mass media encouraged such questioning. Even before the heyday of McCarthy, articles appeared in major magazines with titles such as "How Communists Get That Way," "How the Russians Spied on Their Allies," "Trained to Raise Hell in America: International Lenin School in Moscow," "Communists Penetrate Wall Street," "Why I Broke with the Communists," "Reds Are After Your Child," "How Communists Take Over." Anticommunist, anti-Soviet books glutted bookstores—Victor Kravchenko, *I Choose Freedom,* Hamilton Fish, *The Red Plotters,* Richard Hirsch, *The Soviet Spies,* Louis Budenz, *This Is My Story,* Richard Crossman, ed., *The God That Failed,* to name but a few. *I Led Three Lives,* Herbert Philbrick's story about his role as communist turned FBI informer, was serialized in some 500 newspapers. Hollywood turned out such thrillers as *I Married a Communist, The Red Menace, The Iron Curtain, The Conspirator, Guilty of Treason,* and *I Was a Communist for the FBI.*

The popular image of a communist conveyed by such massive propaganda was that of a nearly superhuman daemon, a devious and highly skilled fiend, the master of techniques of hypnotic intellectual seduction who would be more than a match for ordinary mortals operating under the lawful ways of democracy. Consequently, Americans became quite tolerant of extralegal vigilante violence committed against supposed Reds. Henry Wallace's Progressive party presidential campaign in 1948, falsely labeled a communist movement by both major parties and the press, was constantly harassed. Speakers were heckled, egged, and stoned; meetings were broken up. On one occasion a Wallace supporter, Robert New, was murdered at a public rally. The killer received a three-year sentence for manslaughter.

Similarly, in the summer of 1949, a concert by the black singer Paul Robeson held in Peekskill, New York, to benefit a civil rights organization that had been placed without a hearing on the attorney-general's subversive list, was brutally disrupted. Hundreds of casualties resulted.

No wonder, then, Americans bought some three million copies of Mickey Spillane's 1951 thriller *One Lonely Night*. In this novel the author's gutsy American hero Mike Hammer brags "I killed more people tonight than I have fingers on my hands. I shot them in cold blood and enjoyed

 ## The Human Cost of McCarthyism

The accusations of Senator McCarthy prodded the Federal Bureau of Investigation (FBI) to reach beyond constitutional bounds and investigate the writings, speeches, and thoughts of Americans who might have or who once had Communist sympathies. Friends and relatives of those targeted were pressured to testify against loved ones, immigrants likewise pressured to inform under threat of deportation.

An amazingly large proportion of the victims [of McCarthyism] are elderly. In his comprehensive report, [researcher] Abner Green pointed out that of three hundred non-citizens arrested in deportation proceedings, almost one third—ninety-three in all—are over the age of sixty and have lived in this country an average of forty to fifty years. The kind of sick and aged folk being hauled out of retirement for deportation as a political menace to this country would be ludicrous if it did not entail so much tragedy. Two cardiac patients, Refugio Roman Martinez and Norman Tallentire, died of heart attacks in deportation proceedings. The economist and writer, Lewis Corey, long an anti-Communist, died September 16 at the age of sixty-one in the midst of deportation proceedings begun against him because he was a Communist thirty years ago. In California, a Mrs. Mary Baumert of Elsinore, now seventy-six

every minute of it. I pumped slugs in the nastiest bunch of bastards you ever saw. . . . They were Commies. . . . They were red sons-of-bitches who should have died long ago. . . . They never thought there were people like me in this country. They figured us all to be soft as horse manure and just as stupid."

McCarthy's Laundry List

While the brutal Mike Hammer was fictional, muscular ex-marine Joseph R. McCarthy, the junior senator from Wis-

---

years old, was arrested last month for deportation although she had lived here fifty-one years. In Los Angeles on November 4, Mr. and Mrs. Lars Berg, sixty-nine and sixty-seven respectively, were locked up on Terminal Island for deportation to their native Sweden; they have been American residents since 1904. One Finn arrested for deportation has lived here since he was three months old!

As in the days of the Inquisition, the Immigration and Naturalization Service and the FBI are engaged in using fear to recruit informers, even informers against their own kin. A striking case was that of Francesco Costa of Rochester, New York, arrested for deportation to Italy at the age of eighty-three because he refused to provide information to the Justice Department that could be used to deport his son, Leonard, to Italy. A triple squeeze play was brought to bear on Clarence Hathaway, once editor of the *Daily Worker*. When he declined to be used as an informer, denaturalization proceedings were brought against his wife, Vera. Her brother, William Sanders, fifty-five, an artist who had never engaged in politics, was himself arrested after he refused to give testimony against his sister. Sophie Gerson, wife of Simon W. Gerson, one of those acquitted in the second Smith Act trial of New York Communist leaders, was arrested for denaturalization to punish her husband.

I.F. Stone, *The Haunted Fifties*. New York: Vintage Books, 1969.

consin, was all too real. On February 9, 1950, less than a week after the Fuchs story broke and while Americans were still inflamed over Hiss, China, and the Soviet bomb, McCarthy, holding an old laundry list while addressing the Wheeling Women's Republican Club, announced, "I have here in my hand a list of 205 that were known to the Secretary of State as being members of the Communist party and who, nevertheless, are still working and shaping policy in the State Department." With these words began McCarthy's national anticommunist career. In the following five years he would take the already existing mania to new heights of irrational hysteria.

But it needs to be emphasized again that McCarthy did not create the national paranoia over communism. He merely capitalized on it. His rhetoric and tactics, though extreme, were well within the already established framework of cold war politics. In fact, many Democrats inadvertently furthered McCarthy's cause through their own exaggerated depiction of the communist threat. For example, Truman's last attorney general, J. Howard McGrath, in an address some two months after McCarthy's Wheeling diatribe, claimed: "There are today many Communists in America. They are everywhere—in factories, offices, butcher shops, on street corners, in private business—and each carries in himself the germs of death for society." These communists, he warned, "are busy at work—undermining your Government, plotting to destroy the liberties of every citizen, and feverishly trying, in whatever way they can, to aid the Soviet Union." Such speeches, of course, coincided with McCarthy's claims that the Truman administration was "soft on communism."

From Wheeling on February 9, McCarthy went on to repeat his charges in Salt Lake City the following night and in Reno on February 11, though now claiming 57 as the number of known communists in government. He also sent President Truman an insulting telegram demanding of the man who had already initiated the largest loyalty check in American history that he do something about the communists in the State Department. McCarthy's repetitive charges soon attracted national attention. On February 20, 1950, he brought his show to the floor of the Senate where for nearly six hours he spewed forth accusations. Now he professed to have 81 documented cases of communists in the State Department.

These were grave charges. The Senate responded by establishing a special investigative committee headed by conservative Maryland Democrat Millard Tydings. For several months this committee carefully sifted through evidence, took testimony, ran down leads. Without exception McCarthy's cases proved false. They were based on rumor, gossip, lies. Most had been drawn from old and already discredited files. When the Tydings committee report was made public on July 17, 1950, McCarthy was bluntly exposed for the falsifier he was. "At a time when American blood is again being shed to preserve our dream of freedom," began the report, "we are constrained fearlessly and frankly to call the charges, and the methods employed to give them ostensible validity, what they truly are: a fraud and a hoax. . . . They represent perhaps the most nefarious campaign of half-truths and untruths in the history of this republic. For the first time in our history, we have seen the totalitarian technique of the 'big lie' employed on a sustained basis.". . .

Two years later when Eisenhower's popularity gave the Republicans control of Congress as well as the White House, McCarthy was rewarded with the chairmanship of his own investigative committee.

Smearing Opponents

The Hearst, McCormick, and Scripps-Howard newspapers favorably publicized McCarthy's charges and crusades. The New York *Daily News* and the Dallas *Morning News* also supported him. So too did prominent magazines such as the *Saturday Evening Post, U.S. News & World Report,* and the *American Mercury.* . . . But even papers not ostensibly in McCarthy's camp fostered the notion that the senator was discovering real espionage. In the atmosphere of terror of the time, his fabricated charges were front-page, banner-headline stuff. Denials or complete proof of the falsehood of McCarthy's allegations might eventually appear on page 17, squeezed between two girdle ads. But in the meantime McCarthy would have captured page one with yet another big lie. *New York Times* columnist Peter Kihss finally felt obliged to warn that "the reading public should understand that it is difficult if not impossible to ignore charges by Senator McCarthy just because they are usually proved exaggerated or false."

Published stories the least bit unfavorable to McCarthy evoked the senator's wrath. When the generally pro-McCarthy *Time* magazine ran a slightly censorious article in 1952, McCarthy wrote *Time:* "I am sure you will agree that the policy of *Time* magazine to throw pebbles at communism generally but to then parallel the [American Communist Party newspaper the] *Daily Worker's* smear attack upon individuals who start to dig out dangerous secret Communists, is rendering almost unlimited service to the Communist cause and undermining America." McCarthy harshly attacked reporters regularly critical of him such as Drew Pearson and James Wechsler. In Pearson's case, McCarthy, in addition to his usual verbal abuse (he called Pearson a "Moscow-directed character assassin"), actually kneed the columnist in the groin and punched him about the head when the two accidentally encountered one another in the cloakroom of Washington's Sulgrave Club on December 12, 1950. Though Pearson brought suit against McCarthy, nothing came of it. In fact, McCarthy was able to pressure Adams Hats to stop sponsoring Pearson's popular radio program. Pearson continued to oppose McCarthy. But few other reporters were courageous enough to stand up against the senator's intimidating tactics. The press, therefore, until McCarthy's downfall became evident, was overwhelmingly pro-McCarthy. . . .

Internal Security Act

Democrats should have united to a man against the Wisconsin senator. Time and again he slandered them and their party. In a Charleston, West Virginia, speech he stated: "The hard fact is that those who wear the label—Democrat—wear it with the stain of an historic betrayal." Yet as late as February 1954, the Senate passed an appropriation bill for the continued funding of McCarthy's investigating committee by a vote of 85 to 1. Only Arkansas Democrat William Fulbright dissented. Guilt and fear had undermined the Democrats. Many actually believed some of the reckless charges of having been too lax on the communist issue, and certainly the Hiss case had a demoralizing effect. Others learned too well the lesson of [Congressman] Tyding's defeat [in the 1950 election]. Opposition to McCarthy could result in political suicide. It is not that individual Democrats (and some Republicans, too) failed to attack McCarthy; many did. What was lacking was a sustained, co-ordinated attack of sufficient magnitude to succeed.

More typical of Democratic tactics was the continuation of Truman's 1947 strategy, trying to assert their party's anticommunist credentials. Stevenson, campaigning in 1952, spoke of how effectively the Democrats had exposed the communists "before the junior Senator from Wisconsin suddenly appeared on the scene and began his wild and reckless campaign." Unquestionably this was an attempt by Democratic politicians to co-opt the issue, snatch it from GOP hands, and make it—and especially the power involved—their own. In retrospect it is clear that this tactic only confirmed in the public mind McCarthy's contention that there was a menace. Liberal Democrats, very fearful of being considered fellow-travelers [Communist sympathizers], often went to extremes on the communist issue. Hubert Humphrey actually introduced a bill to outlaw the Communist party altogether. Paul Douglas, the liberal Illinois senator, supported Humphrey, claiming that Republicans kept the Communist party in existence "to smear Democrats like myself. We liberals must destroy the Communists if this dirty game is to stop." Such a liberalism, of course, was simply self-defeating.

The anticommunist political atmosphere of the time was

evidenced by the wide range of witch-hunting activity and legislation not directly attributable to the Wisconsin senator. In 1951 Congress overwhelmingly passed the McCarran Internal Security Act. This required communist and so-called communist-front organizations to register with the government and to clearly label all their mail and literature as communist. This act, by establishing a five-member Subversive Activities Control Board with the authority to investigate the thoughts and beliefs of citizens, sanctified internal repression. Its most totalitarian provision was first proposed by Humphrey, Douglas, and other liberals. The board set up concentration camps and authorized the government to lock up communists and other suspected subversives any time a national emergency was proclaimed.

In addition to McCarthy's own Government Operations Committee, which he illegally used for probing supposed subversive activities, two other congressional committees—HUAC and the Senate Internal Security Committee—were also active in the Red-hunting business. The FBI and the CIA naturally were involved too. Then in April 1953, President Eisenhower bestirred himself to issue Executive Order 10450, establishing a loyalty program even more sweeping and strict than Truman's 1947 measure. By Ike's order, all new government employees and workers in firms with government contracts regardless of position were to be investigated. Any derogatory information, no matter what its source (always kept secret), was grounds for dismissal. Furthermore, all those cleared by field investigations during Truman's administration had to undergo another full investigation, during which they were suspended without pay. . . .

McCarthy's Downfall

After nearly five years of irresponsible actions—forcing from the State Department the only knowledgeable Far Eastern experts, weakening the Voice of America, purging from United States overseas libraries books by Theodore Dreiser, Archibald MacLeish, Arthur Miller, Arthur Schlesinger, Jr., and hundreds of other "dangerous" authors, disrupting the army base at Fort Monmouth, New Jersey, defaming thousands—McCarthy fell from grace. The downfall began with a 35-day Senate investigation into alleged attempts to gain preferential treatment from the army for his young assistant, Private G. David Schine. The televised hearings gave millions of Americans the opportunity to see for themselves the bludgeoning manner of the unprincipled communist hunter as he attacked the army's dignified top brass. His popularity lessened. Even before the hearings closed, the Senate got up the nerve to start an inquiry of its own into McCarthy's conduct as a senator. Finally on December 2, 1954, his colleagues by a vote of 67 to 22 condemned him. Though he retained all his senatorial privileges, McCarthy's power did not survive censure. Always a heavy drinker, he imbibed more after this. His health deteriorated, and on May 2, 1957, he died.

Learning to Love the Bomb

Margot A. Henriksen

Relatively new, nuclear weapons and the threat they posed to other nations and to the United States were constantly in the public's mind. While the government was building these incredibly destructive weapons, Americans wrestled with the moral implications of using them. Official propaganda was designed to minimize such concerns, regularly describing nuclear bombs as harmless, even lovable. Euphemistic language described radiation levels as "sunshine units" and small nuclear bombs as "kitten bombs." Because prolonged conflict was unlikely in the event of nuclear war, hydrogen bombs were called "humanitarian bombs" or "clean bombs." In this selection, Margot A. Henriksen, associate professor of history at the University of Hawaii, describes this propaganda.

That very exhilaration that most postwar Americans felt about America's atomic power made expressions of guilt and remorse about the atom bomb seem traitorous, a blow against the simple and innocent values that World War II had secured. For this reason most Americans accepted the bomb openly, or at the very least they accepted it in silence and apathy. It was for this reason also that the scientists' organized antibomb sentiment failed to find a wide audience. Having just fought a world war for the protection of

Excerpted from *Dr. Strangelove's America: Society and Culture in the Atomic Age,* by Margot A. Henriksen. Copyright ©1997 by the Regents of the University of California. Reprinted with permission from the University of California Press.

a particular American way of life, nationalistic Americans were not inclined to express sympathy for the scientists' internationalist ideas about the control of atomic energy and atomic weapons. Plans for world government or the international control of atomic energy—whether generated by nuclear scientists or United States and United Nations proposals . . . found little support from Americans or from the suspicious governments of the United States and the Soviet Union. The failure of these far-sighted plans did not mean, however, that all moral qualms and mistrust of atomic power evaporated. The sense of knowing sin and the fear of the evil of atomic knowledge first expressed by select scientists received sympathetic hearing in the cold war culture of dissent (even if scientists themselves were sometimes treated with little sympathy). The doubt-filled products of popular culture questioned President Truman's notion of the atom bomb as a "weapon of peace" and instead focused on the evil repercussions of America's policy of atomic invincibility, from its capacity for apocalyptic destruction to its incompatibility with those "concepts of democracy and political morality which had been our wartime heritage."

Physicist Philip Morrison, who had devoted years of labor to the Manhattan Project, [offered his] view of the bomb's distortion of democratic political morality. According to Morrison, America's postwar atomic arsenals, their institutional support systems, and their unimaginable scale of destructiveness constituted the evil legacy of World War II:

> This is the legacy of World War II, a direct legacy of Hitler. When we beat the Nazis, we emulated them. I include myself. I became callous to death. I became willing to risk everything on war and peace. I followed my leaders enthusiastically and rather blindly. . . . We fought the war to stop fascism. But it transformed the societies that opposed fascism. They took on some of its attributes.

While there is a certain measure of dramatics in such a statement, the United States government's reliance on atomic weapons with their potential for genocide and the government's obsession with protecting its atomic secrets did support the charge that America had learned to emulate its enemies in order to fight them—from Hitler's callousness about death to the Soviet Union's maintenance of domestic tranquillity through the repression of its populace. . . .

Scientists Protest

Faced with the cold war and an aggressive Soviet Union, the United States chose first to strengthen its atomic arsenal and then in the urgent and frantic atmosphere surrounding the Soviet atomic explosion to develop the hydrogen bomb as a new counterforce against the Soviets. The hydrogen bomb exponentially increased the destructive and genocidal potential of America's weapons arsenal, and the physicists involved in the Atomic Energy Commission (AEC) decision on the hydrogen bomb futilely attempted to block this new nuclear compromise with evil. In 1949 the General Advisory Committee to the AEC, led by J. Robert Oppenheimer, strenuously objected to the development of the "super bomb." The majority report of the committee stated its opposition:

> We base our recommendation on our belief that the extreme dangers to mankind inherent in the proposal wholly outweigh any military advantage that could come from this development. Let it be clearly realized that this is a super weapon; it is in a totally different category from an atomic bomb. The reason for developing such super bombs would be to have the capacity to devastate a vast area with a single bomb. Its use would involve a decision to slaughter a vast number of civilians. . . . If super bombs work at all, there is no inherent limit in the destructive power that may be attained with them. Therefore, a super bomb might become a weapon of genocide.

The minority opinion report objected to the hydrogen bomb even more vehemently; physicists Enrico Fermi and I.I. Rabi insisted that "it is necessarily an evil thing considered in any light" and they urged "the President of the United States to tell the American public, and the world, that we think it wrong on fundamental ethical principles to initiate a program of development of such a weapon."

While the public had little access to these ethical arguments, at least until the hydrogen bomb was tested and until Oppenheimer lost his security clearance in part as a result of his moral qualms about the H-bomb, an uneasiness about the decaying political morality associated with America's quest for atomic invincibility did surface in certain corners of the culture. The government's compromise with atomic evils led to certain ethical compromises in the government's relations with its citizens. In order to protect its atomic policies and secure those policies from widespread criticism, the government engaged in secrecy and deception, instituting internal security programs that captured spies and all sorts of communist allies and quieted atomic dissenters. The government had legitimate security concerns in this new world, but its pursuit of internal security and atomic secrecy went beyond the bounds of reason, creating an atmosphere of suspicion that eventually also encompassed the government and its security forces.

Eisenhower's "Atoms for Peace"

By the time Eisenhower took office in 1953, it appeared that the government's atomic policies had corroded its sense of honesty and democratic decency. In a January 1953 advisory group report to Eisenhower on the possibility of disarmament, the scientists' group, led again by Oppenheimer, argued that too many nuclear weapons already existed and that the American people needed to be made aware of the dangers of these weapons. Oppenheimer called for "Operation Candor," in which "candor on the part of the officials, the representatives, of the people of their country," was forthcoming. "Operation Candor" explicitly deplored the government's failure to share information with the public, and even though Eisenhower seemed open to atomic honesty, he nonetheless resisted true candor. Impressed by Oppenheimer's image of "two scorpions in a bottle" and by the mutual and massive destruction implicit in any atomic confrontation between the United States and the Soviet Union, Eisenhower nonetheless did not want the full and despairing truth known; he did not "want to scare the country to death. Can't we find some hope?"

Eisenhower opted for a compromise between candor and hope, and he delivered his "Atoms for Peace" speech to the United Nations in December 1953. The speech addressed the deadly cold war scenario in which "two atomic colossi are doomed malevolently to eye each other indefinitely across a trembling world," but Eisenhower also put forth a tentative plan for an international agency that would stockpile uranium and fissionable materials in order "to serve the peaceful pursuits of mankind," in order "to serve the needs rather than the fears of mankind." Eisenhower enunciated a message of peace and he promised that the United States would "devote its entire heart and mind to find the way by which the miraculous inventiveness of man shall not be dedicated to his death, but consecrated to his life." Despite good intentions little resulted from this plan, which went the way of most early plans for international control of atomic energy. Eisenhower's administration stopped talking of candor or "atoms for peace."

The Not So *Lucky Dragon*

The government's quick return to a confidential policy was evident after the March 1954 hydrogen bomb tests on Bikini atoll. The Bikini blasts proved twice as powerful as expected and a Japanese fishing boat—ironically named the *Lucky Dragon*—lying well outside the stated danger zone was coated with the ashes of radioactive fallout. The burned and contaminated crewmen arrived in Japan complaining of illness, and when their radiation sickness was diagnosed and the cause discovered, the resulting furor forced the American government to respond. Washington, however, offered duplicitous arguments and denials. Popular periodicals like *Newsweek* and *New Republic* reported on the *Lucky Dragon* and the government's equivocation, the *New Republic* leveling its sights particularly on Lewis Strauss, head of the Atomic Energy Commission, who had made an official statement on the *Lucky Dragon:*

> But, said Strauss, reports on the range of dangerous radioactivity were exaggerated; the *Lucky Dragon* must have been "well within" the forbidden area, and its crewmen obviously had been burned by a chemical fall-out, not poisoned by a radioactive one. This has remained the official American attitude, although every fact so far uncovered shows it to be a willful minimization of a new danger which must eventually condition all thinking about both the use of and defense against the super-bomb.

Preparing for Atomic War

Susan Jonas and Marilyn Nissenson

As Susan Jonas and Marilyn Nissenson, authors of *Going Going Gone: Vanishing Americana* point out in the following selection, one of the largest nuclear weapons buildups in history occurred during the 1950s. The prospect of atomic war was on everyone's mind. In 1951, Harry Truman was forced to acknowledge the possibility of American nuclear annihilation when he created the Federal Civil Defense Administration (CDA). The agency recommended that average citizens dig bomb shelters or devise and stock one in their basements. In response, popular magazines such as *Life* made such ludicrous claims as the statistical likelihood that ninety-seven out of one hundred people would survive an atom bomb attack if they were in a shelter.

In 1950, the invasion of South Korea by the Communist North Korean army forced Americans to face the possibility of World War III and total nuclear annihilation. Images of the suffering inflicted five years earlier by the atomic bombs dropped on Hiroshima and Nagasaki were still vivid. The popular press pictured American cities devastated by atomic attack with transportation paralysed, power and food supplies destroyed, hundreds of thousands of casualties, and no way to get help for the sick and dying.

Acknowledging the "grim new reality," President Harry

Excerpted from *Going, Going, Gone: Vanishing Americana,* by Susan Jonas and Marilyn Nissenson. Copyright ©1994 by Susan Jonas and Marilyn Nissenson. Reprinted with permission from Chronicle Books, San Francisco.

Truman created the Federal Civil Defense Administration in January 1951. Many of the materials it produced were intended to prepare schoolchildren for atomic war, to "alert, not alarm" them. Teachers and parents were urged not to become unduly emotional at the prospect of Russian attack. The national PTA urged a soothing, "positive mental health program" in response to atomic anxiety. The bomb's worst effects, such as traumatic injuries, shock, burns, radiation sickness, and death, were to be played down.

Throughout the 1950s many cities staged regular air-raid drills. Civil defense officials tested all 741 sirens in New York City every month. A one-minute alert was followed by a warbling sound that meant "take cover." Schools, especially in target cities like New York, Los Angeles, Chicago, and Philadelphia, conducted "duck-and-cover" drills. When the teacher suddenly shouted "drop!" all the children would kneel, hands clasped behind their necks and their faces shielded.

The FCDA circulated a comic book featuring Bert the Turtle. Bert said: "You have learned to take care of yourself in many ways—to cross streets safely—and what to do in case of fire. . . . BUT the atomic bomb is a new danger . . . things will get knocked down all over town. . . . You must be ready to protect yourself." Bert warned children to "DUCK to avoid things flying through the air." With his head retracted into his shell, he urged them to "COVER to keep from getting cut or even badly burned."

Many school districts distributed special student identification, modeled after military dog tags. The tags were designed to help civil defense workers identify lost or dead children in event of nuclear attack. By 1952 New York City had issued two and a half million free dog tags to public, parochial, and private schoolchildren.

"Die, Dig, or Get Out"

In 1954 Lewis Strauss, chairman of the Atomic Energy Commission, revealed the existence of a new weapon, the H-bomb, which could incinerate an entire city. The H-bomb made obsolete all previous civil defense plans based on estimates of A-bomb damage. The only response, said one civil defense administrator in 1954, is to "die, dig, or get out." Digging bomb-proof shelters throughout the country would have cost more than the Eisenhower administration was willing to spend, so plans were made to evacuate cities on the basis of a four- to six-hour warning of a bomber attack.

It was later revealed that the federal government was willing to shelter a select few. A secret concrete-and-steel bunker for members of Congress was built in 1958 into a hill adjacent to the luxurious Greenbrier resort in White Sulphur Springs, West Virginia, 250 miles southwest of Washington. The government also built quarters at Mount Weather in Virginia, where the president, members of the Supreme Court, and other top officials could ride out the emergency.

In the late 1950s, intercontinental ballistic missiles armed with nuclear warheads put an end to evacuation planning. ICBMs could cover the five thousand miles between Washington and Moscow in thirty minutes or less, which barely allowed anyone enough time to get out of town or take shelter. "Civil defense is dead, as of right now," declared a writer in the September 28, 1957, issue of the *Nation*. "To all the people who have been worrying because the stumbling procedures of the FCDA left them uncertain and unprepared, the ICBM brings a paradoxical note of cheer: you don't have to worry anymore."

Backyard Bomb Shelters

The Rand Corporation, however, predicted that civil defense could limit carnage even in a nuclear exchange. An effective combination of military and civil defense would give half the population a good chance of survival in a thermonuclear war, which, though catastrophic, would not wipe out all life. Rand recommended that people spend one or two hundred dollars of their own money to build a family fallout shelter. . . .

What to Do in Case of Atomic Attack

Federal and state governments issued many brochures with instructions for surviving nuclear attack in an effort to quell the fears of the general public. Although it seems ridiculous today, people were taught that they would be protected from the debris generated by a ten-megaton bomb burning hot as the sun if they ducked and covered their heads or if they lay face down in the street.

WHAT YOU SHOULD DO IN CASE OF ATOMIC ATTACK

Keep calm. If there is time, get to shelter at once. If no underground shelter is close by, get into the ground floor of a near-by building or even stand in a doorway if nothing better is available. If you see the bomb flash and there is no cover of any kind within a step or two, drop to the street or gutter, turn away from the flash, and close eyes tightly. Cover your head, face, neck, arms and other exposed areas of the body. If you are indoors, turn off all appliances, such as electric toasters, irons, stoves, etc. Get into the core of your building and under a desk or table if there isn't time to get to the basement. Lie face downward and out of line with windows. After the burst tie handkerchief over mouth if area is contaminated.

WHAT YOU SHOULD NOT DO

Don't telephone. Don't turn on water after blast, unless to fight fire. Don't eat or drink in a contaminated area. Don't use metal goods in a contaminated zone. Don't touch things after ground or water burst. Don't try to drive your car. Don't get excited or excite others.

—"You and the Atomic Bomb," New York State Civil Defense Commission, 1951.

Quoted in Susan Jonas and Marilyn Nissenson, *Going Going Gone: Vanishing Americana*. San Francisco: Chronicle, 1994.

"Fallout shelter fever" hit America. Sporting goods stores did a brisk business in camping equipment for use in basement shelters. The sales pitch at the Prince Georges County Shopping Plaza outside Washington, D.C., was typical. A bass voice over the loudspeaker announced, "This is condition Red." A siren wailed; a bomb exploded. A male voice screamed, "My wife, my children." Pause. "If I'd only listened to Civil Defense, I'd be in a shelter now." This commercial message was designed to attract attention to a closed-circuit TV view of a nine-by-ten-foot cinderblock basement shelter which could protect a family of four for a week before they ran out of supplies. . . .

No one knows how many shelters were sold—maybe as many as two hundred thousand. But by the end of 1962, the threat of nuclear war eased. One Detroit dealer advertised "Fallout Shelters While They Last" and slashed prices down to $100. He tried to give one away. A writer was willing to use the shelter as a study. A woman wanted it for a toolshed. A businessman in Beirut thought it would make a nice beach house. "But almost nobody wanted it as a

Fear of a nuclear attack led many Americans to invest in underground bomb shelters.

shelter," the dealer said. A Michigan farmer finally hauled it off, because he thought it might be useful in the event of a tornado.

In December 1961 the *Washington Daily News* summed up the state of civil defense in the early 1960s: "C is for confusion; D is for Dilemma." People feared that shelter programs emphasized surviving war rather than averting it. Others complained that the government's every-man-for-himself approach brought out the worst in human nature. There were serious debates about whether or not the head of a household had the right to gun down any outsider who tried to get into the family shelter. The average person couldn't afford to build one and, in any case, thought the nation should be responsible for each citizen's personal defense.

As time passed, speculation centered on the horrors of nuclear winter: subfreezing temperatures, darkness at noon, worldwide fallout, and partial destruction of the ozone layer. As Jonathan Schell wrote in *The Fate of the Earth,* "The vulnerability of the environment is the last word in the argument against the usefulness of shelters: there is no hole big enough to hide all of nature in." Although the preoccupation with nuclear war continued, and national defense remained a major issue, civil defense ceased to be a viable solution. No one wanted to live on in a devastated and radioactive world.

CHAPTER 3

The Racial Divide

The Death of Emmett Till

Henry Hampton and Steve Fayer

In 1954 the Supreme Court struck down separate-but-equal laws that enforced racial segregation in the South. When blacks tried to exercise their new rights, however, white people began a wave of violence against blacks. Blacks who tried to vote or attend white schools were murdered. This violence was largely ignored by the national press until the murder of Chicago-born African American teenager Emmett Till in 1955 in Money, Mississippi. The trial of the white men who killed him riveted national attention on the violent racism of the segregated South. Henry Hampton was the executive producer of the PBS documentary on the civil rights movement *Eyes on the Prize.* Steve Fayer is an Emmy Award–winning series writer. In this selection, the authors focus on the impact Emmett Till's death had on the civil rights movement.

On August 20, 1955, Emmett Till, a fourteen-year-old from Chicago's South Side, almost missed the train that would carry him to a summer visit with relatives in the Mississippi Delta. Emmett, nicknamed Bo, was supposed to meet his seventeen-year-old cousin, Curtis Jones, at LaSalle Street station. Young Till didn't show up at LaSalle Street, but with only seconds to spare, out of breath and stammering with excitement, he boarded the train at Englewood, more than seven miles away.

Excerpted from *Voices of Freedom: An Oral History of the Civil Rights Movement From the 1950s Through the 1980s,* by Henry Hampton and Steve Fayer, with Sarah Flynn. Copyright ©1990 by Blackside, Inc. Reprinted with permission from Bantam Books, a division of Random House, Inc.

In the forty years since World War I began, Chicago's black population had grown from some forty thousand to half a million. Many blacks had moved up from the South, seeking jobs and a better way of life. Of those, 75 percent hailed from Mississippi. Emmett Till was part of the emigrant community and was closing the circle that summer, traveling back to his family's home place.

Executed for Exercising Their Rights

Money, Mississippi, was a dusty crossroads, population fifty-five, with the Tallahatchie River at its back door. Emmett's mother had warned the boy to mind his manners with whites down there. No one expected a fourteen-year-old to be in mortal danger, but anyone black had to be careful. More than five hundred black people had been lynched in the state since these statistics were first compiled in 1882. Thousands more racially motivated murders were never officially reported. Now, in the summer of 1955, the death toll was beginning to build again, particularly in the Delta, the northwest corner of the state, where Money was located.

In some Delta counties, blacks constituted 80 percent of the population, and the outnumbered whites were bent on intimidating any blacks who wanted access to a better education or to the ballot box. Three months before Emmett's trip, the Reverend George Lee from the Delta town of Belzoni was killed by a shotgun blast to the face. Local authorities ruled his death a traffic accident. Lee had been the first black to register to vote in the county.

On August 13, just a week before Emmett's arrival, Lamar Smith, a black man who had voted in the state's Democratic primary earlier in the month, was shot to death at high noon in front of the courthouse in Brookhaven. Again, there were no arrests.

For almost seventy years, the U.S. Supreme Court had supported southern insistence on second-class citizenship for blacks. With the *Brown v. Board of Education* decision in 1954, the Court signaled that it was changing its position regarding the legality of segregating black and white schoolchildren. Reaction in the South was swift, particularly in Mississippi. Leaders of the white supremacist Ku Klux Klan exhorted their followers to resist the "mongrelization" of the white race. White Citizens' Councils were formed to exert political and economic pressure on black activists and their white sympathizers. . . . Ten years after the end of World War II, many whites in the Delta felt that Mississippi was now in another war to protect its way of life.

Emmett arrived in Mississippi with his cousin Curtis Jones on August 21, 1955. . . .

An Innocent Remark

[Curtis Jones continues with the story]: [Moses Wright] my grandfather in Mississippi was a preacher. He had a church and he had a little raggedy '41 Ford, if I'm not mistaken. And he took all of us to church [the day the trouble started . . .]. While he was in the pulpit preaching, [Emmett and I] get the car and drive to Money. Anyway, we went into this store to buy some candy. Before Emmett went in, he had shown the boys round his age some picture of some white kids that he had graduated from school with, female and male. He told the boys who had gathered round this store—there must have been maybe ten to twelve youngsters there—that one of the girls was his girlfriend. So one of the local boys said, "Hey, there's a white girl in that store there. I bet you won't go in there and talk to her." So Emmett went in there. When he was leaving out the store, after buying some candy, he told her, "Bye, baby."

I was sitting out there playing checkers with this older man. Next thing I know, one of the boys came up to me and said, "Say, man, you got a crazy cousin. He just went in there and said 'Bye, baby' to that white woman." This man I was playing checkers with jumped straight up and said, "Boy, you better get out of here. That lady'll come out of that store and blow your brains off."

It was kind of funny to us. We hopped in the car and drove back to the church. . . .

The next day we was telling some youngsters what had happened, but they had heard about it. One girl was telling us that we better get out of there 'cause when that lady's husband come back gonna be big trouble. We didn't tell our grandfather. If we had told our grandfather, I'm sure he would have gotten us out of there. That was Wednesday. So that Thursday passed, nothing happened. Friday passed, nothing happened. Saturday, nothing happened. So we forgot about it.

Kidnapped in the Night

Saturday night we went to town. . . . We must have stayed there till approximately three o'clock that morning. We returned and . . . it must have been about three-thirty, I was awakened by a group of men in the house. . . . When they came, my grandfather answered the door and they asked him did he have three boys in there from Chicago? And he stated yes. He said I got my two grandsons and a nephew. So they told him get the one who did the talking. My grandmother was scared to death. She was trying to protect Bo. They told her get back in bed. One of the guys struck her with a shotgun side of the head. When I woke up the next morning, I thought it was a dream.

I went to the porch and my grandfather was sitting on the porch. I asked him, "Poppa, did they bring Bo back?" He said, "No." He said, "I hope they didn't kill that boy." And that's when I got kind of scared.

I asked him, "Ain't you going to call the police?" He said, "No, I can't call the police. They told me that if I call the sheriff they was going to kill everybody in this house." So I told him, I say, *"I'll* call."

That happened Sunday.

When Curtis Jones called the sheriff that Sunday, he also placed a call to his mother, Willie Mae Jones, back in Chicago. She in turn got in touch with Emmett's mother, Mamie Till Bradley, a thirty-three-year-old schoolteacher.

Willie Mae was hysterical. I could barely get any sense out

of her. But I finally pieced out that Emmett had been taken from her father's house. I said, "Mama, Willie Mae said someone had taken Emmett from Poppa Mose's house." Well, Mother comprehended the situation immediately. And that of course alerted me that there was real danger.

By Wednesday we knew. It was beyond the shadow of a doubt—the thing had really come fallin' in place. We knew about the men who had taken Emmett. We knew the alleged crime. We knew that something was highly amiss that Emmett hadn't turned up by then. . . . We knew the situation was serious, and we just couldn't name it—that he had been killed. You just couldn't put it into words, but deep down in our hearts we were fearing that.

> Based on information that Mose Wright and Crosby Smith gave the sheriff, two men were arrested for kidnapping— Roy Bryant, husband of the woman in the store, and his half brother, J.W. Milam. That Wednesday, Emmett Till's body was discovered in the Tallahatchie River. A cotton gin fan was tied to his neck with barbed wire. Milam and Bryant now faced murder charges. . . .

Emmett's Mother Wants the World to See

[Emmett's mother continues] I understand the order came from the sheriff's office to bury that body just as soon as you can. And they didn't even allow it to go to a funeral parlor and be dressed. He was in a pine box. Well, we got busy. We called the governor, we called the sheriff, we called Crosby, my mother's brother. We called everybody we thought would be able to stop the burial of that body. I wanted that body. I demanded that body because my thoughts were, I had to see it, to make sure, because I'd be wondering even now who was buried in Mississippi. I had to know that was Emmett. Between Crosby and the sheriff in Mississippi who went with him and the undertaker here who contacted the undertaker there, we were able to stop the burial.

After the body arrived I knew that I had to look and see

and make sure it was Emmett. That was when I decided that I wanted the whole world to see what I had seen. There was no way I could describe what was in that box. No way. And I just wanted the world to see.

> The boy's body was so mutilated that Mose Wright had been able to identify Emmett only by the ring on his finger. The black press was outraged. *Jet* magazine ran a photograph of the corpse that Mamie Till Bradley had resolved all the world should see. Her son's face was swollen and disfigured. He had been beaten severely. One eye was gouged out, and one side of his forehead was crushed. A bullet was lodged in his skull.
>
> The *Chicago Defender,* one of the country's largest national black weeklies, gave the Till case and the open-casket funeral prominent coverage. The story of the lynching also received unusual attention in the national white media, with newsreel and television cameras on the scene in the Delta. . . .

Press Coverage from Up North

Simeon Booker, [a reporter from *Jet* magazine, offers his perspective]: The unusual thing was, it was the first time the daily—meaning white—media took an interest in something like this. I remember one of the jokes among our press corps down there was that, hell, they'd go lookin' for Till's body, they would find bodies of a lotta other blacks who'd just been thrown in the river. Because that was the custom, that was the procedure.

Well, after it broke in Chicago and when the boy's mother demanded that the body be brought back, they had thousands that viewed that body, and that really brought it to the international circuit.

When [Charles] Diggs [one of the first black congressmen since the nineteenth century] went down to that trial those blacks had never seen a black congressman. In fact, many of them never knew there was a black congressman, because they didn't have any communication, have any black newspapers down there, they didn't have any radio or anything that gave them information about what was going on outside of Mississippi.

The National News Association, a black wire service, sent reporter James Hicks to cover the trial. Like the other black reporters, Hicks stayed in Mound Bayou, an all-black town about twelve miles from Sumner. There he met Dr. T.R.M. Howard, a physician who earlier that summer had organized a voting rights rally attended by thousands of black people.

James Hicks: A Reporter's Account

Dr. Howard, I'll never forget him. He was a prominent man. Having made his money down there, they, the white folks, looked at him as, I think, the nearest thing "like us.". . .

I asked him, "Are they going to arrest these men? When are they going to sentence them? You think they'll get the chair?" And he said, "Chair, are you kidding?" He said, "I can tell you this. A white man in Mississippi will get no more of a sentence for killing a black person as he would for killing a deer out of season."

He was saying around that this was just the worst thing. So he became a target. Howard saw that it was time for him to go. They had threatened him. So I said, "I'll drive you."

He had a lot of money and he put it in a pillow slip, in cash, with his valuables. We put it in the back of this you-drive-it car. I drove him to Memphis and he flew on to Chicago. . . .

I had covered courts all over this nation, but I never saw anything like the Till case before. First of all, it was a segregated courtroom, and all the white veterans in town were deputized. The press table was denied to blacks. We had to sit at a bridge table far off from the jury, whereas the white press sat right under the judge and the jury, right up front at a reserved section. The laxity in the courtroom was something you couldn't imagine. I mean, they drank beer in the jury box. . . .

Somebody had said that Mose Wright had told them from the git-go that he wanted to testify. He wanted to tell how these people got Emmett Till out of his house that night. All the people in Mound Bayou were saying, "Look, this is it. This man gets up there and identifies J.W. Milam and this other man, Bryant, we don't know what's going to happen. His life won't be worth a dime if he testifies against these two white men." We had been told that this was going to happen, this was a point when the stuff would hit the fan. We black reporters devised our own plan. We were seated in this Jim Crow setup, near a window. On this particular day, every able-bodied white man you saw in the courtroom had a .45 or a .38 strung on him. . . .

When Uncle Mose testified, electricity came over the courtroom. This elderly, gray-haired man sitting up there. The prosecutor said, "Now, Uncle Mose, I am going to ask you, is it a fact that two men came to your house? Now what did they say?"

"They asked, 'You have a nigger here from Chicago?'"

And he told them, "My little nephew is here from Chicago."

"And what did they say then?"

"He ask me where he was, and I said he was in there in the bed 'cause it was nighttime, and so they said get him up. I got him up and then he, they took him away and they said, 'I'm going to take this nigger with us.' I couldn't do anything."

The key point came when they said to him, "I'm going to ask you to look around in the courtroom and see if you see any man here that came to you and knocked on your door that night." And so this old man—I mean, talk about courage—he looked around and in his broken English he said, "Dar he," and he pointed so straight at J.W. Milam. It was like history in that courtroom. It was like electricity in that courtroom. The judge, he was pounding on his gavel and he was saying "Order, order," like that. There was a terrific tension in the courtroom but nothing happened. . . .

The trial lasted five days. In addition to Mose Wright, two other black witnesses took the stand: Willie Reed, who testified he had seen Till in the back of Milam's pickup truck and heard a beating in Milam's barn, and Reed's aunt, Amanda Bradley, who had heard the beating victim cry out, "Momma, Lord have mercy, Lord have mercy." In spite of the eyewitness testimony, the all-white jury returned a verdict of not guilty, having deliberated for one hour. The black witnesses were all moved quickly out of state for their own protection by Medgar Evers, James Hicks, Congressman Diggs, and others.

Two months after the trial, William Bradford Huie, a white journalist and novelist from Alabama, met with one of the several attorneys who had defended Milam and Bryant.

William Bradford Huie: A Journalist's Perspective

Forty or fifty reporters from all over the world had been down there, a highly publicized trial, and because nothing had been established since the trial, all kinds of rumors were being published as truth about great congregations of white men who had beaten somebody in a barn or something. So I told John Whitten [Milam and Bryant's attorney], "John, the truth, whatever the truth is, ought to be told." And I said, "I assume these two white men that you defended—."

And he said, "Well, you know that we all defended them. All the attorneys in town defended them." He said, "You know, my clients, some of them were interested in it. They wanted me to defend them, and in a sense I could charge them a little extra—I'm talking about farm equipment companies and that sort of thing—to defend these boys."

And I said, "Well, I assume they killed the boy, didn't they?"

And John Whitten looked at me and he says, "You know, Bill, I don't know whether they did it or not. I never asked them."

I said, "You mean you defended them in court for a crime here, and you never questioned them?"

He says, "I didn't want to know. Because my wife kept asking me if they killed him. And I kept telling her no."

And he says, "I didn't want them to tell me that they did, because then I'd have to tell my wife, or tell her a lie, so I didn't even want to know."

And I said, "Well, did any of them?"

And he said, "No, none of us questioned them. See, all we did was defend them, which the community wanted us to do."

I said, "Well, John, I want these two men to come in here and tell me the truth, because I think it's the best thing. They're not in jeopardy any longer and I don't see why they shouldn't. I want to make a film about it. And so I'm willing to buy what we call portrayal rights, and I'm willing to pay four thousand dollars for their portrayal rights if they'll come in here and tell me the truth.". . .

I met Milam and Bryant. We had this strange situation. We're meeting in the library of this law firm. Milam and Bryant are sitting on one side of the table, John Whitten and I sitting on the other side. I'm not doing the questioning. Their own lawyer is doing the questioning. And he's never heard their story. Not once. He becomes as interested in the story as I am. . . .

Milam did most of the talking. Now remember, he's older. Milam was then thirty-five or thirty-six. He was a first lieutenant in the U.S. Army Reserve at that time. And so Milam was a bit more articulate than Bryant was. Bryant did some talking, particularly when they talked about what they were told had happened in the store. But J.W. Milam did the killing. He fired the shot when they took Till down on the river and killed him.

They did not intend to kill him when they went and got him. They killed him because he boasted of having a white girl and showed them the pictures of a white girl in Chicago. They had him in the car trying to scare him and that sort of thing for about three hours. Young Till, he never realized the danger he was in, he never knew. I'm quite sure that he never thought these two men would kill him. Maybe he's in such a strange environment he really doesn't know what he's up against. It seems to a rational mind today, it seems impossible that they could have killed him. But J.W. Milam looked up at me and said, "Well, when he told me about this white girl he had," he says, "my friend, that's what this war's about down here now. That's what we got to fight to protect." And he says, "I just looked at him and I said, 'Boy, you ain't never going to see the sun come up again.'"

They were told that they had inherited a way of life. They were told that for a young black man to put his hand sexually on a white woman was something that could not be allowed. They were told that with the beginning of the Supreme Court decision this was a war.

A Sad and Terrible Time

Will Campbell, [a minister at the University of Mississippi, describes what happened to the murderers:] I was the director of religious life at the time, at the University of Mississippi. I knew that whoever had committed this murder would never be convicted. But the two men who were charged with this murder were at the time heroes. Now the strange part of it is, as soon as the trial was over, Mr. William Bradford Huie wrote a story for *Look* magazine . . . where they said, Yes, we took him down there and we beat him and then killed him and threw him in the Tallahatchie River. Those people were nobodies after that. They were disgraced. Which is a strange dichotomy in southern society, that while they were being accused of this crime, we have to rally to their defense and take up money and hire lawyers and all the rest. But then when it's over, "Look, why did you have to disgrace us like that? Now get out of town, we really don't want to see you again."

> For several years after her son's death, Mamie Bradley traveled the country speaking for the NAACP [National Association for the Advancement of Colored People].

Myrlie Evers [wife of NAACP director Medgar Evers, relates people's feelings after Till was murdered:] I bled for Emmett Till's mother. When she came to Mississippi and appeared at the mass meetings, I know how everyone just poured out their hearts to her, went into their pockets when people had only two or three pennies, and gave that—some way to say that we bleed for you, we hurt for you, we are so sorry what happened to Emmett.

It was a sad and terrible time. And perhaps it's too bad to have to say that sometimes it takes those kinds of things to happen, to help a people become stronger and to eliminate the fear so that they have to speak out and do something.

The Montgomery Bus Boycott

Rosa Parks, with Gregory J. Reed

In a first person narrative that dramatically retells her involvement, Rosa Parks gives a recounting of the Montgomery Bus Boycott in this selection. Although the Supreme Court ordered school desegregation in 1954, blacks in the South continued to suffer segregation in restaurants, movie theaters, public bathrooms, public transportation, and elsewhere. On December 1, 1955, an African American woman named Rosa Parks refused to give up her bus seat to a white man in Montgomery, Alabama. This act of righteous defiance sparked a movement that ultimately abolished racial segregation laws in the South.

After Parks refused to move to the back of the bus, she was arrested. The next day, twenty black ministers organized a bus boycott in Montgomery. Over thirty-five thousand flyers were printed and distributed by students and other volunteers. The flyers were circulated secretly because people were afraid of losing their jobs or getting lynched.

On Monday, December 5, the buses were empty. That night, thousands of people gathered in churches to rally against segregation. A new minister in town, twenty-six-year-old Martin Luther King Jr., gave a fiery speech to thousands of boycotters inside a church. Hundreds more listened through loudspeakers out on the street. For thirteen months, empty buses rolled through the streets of Montgomery.

Rosa Parks is the cofounder of the Rosa and Raymond Parks Institute for Self-Development and is recognized as the "mother of the modern-day civil rights movement." Gregory J. Reed is an attorney and the author of eight books.

The custom for getting on the bus for black persons in Montgomery in 1955 was to pay at the front door, get off the bus, and then re-enter through the back door to find a seat. On the buses, if white persons got on, the colored would move back if the white section was filled. Black people could not sit in the same row with white people. They could not even sit across the aisle from each other. Some customs were humiliating, and this one was intolerable since we were the majority of the ridership.

On Thursday evening, December 1, I was riding the bus home from work. A white man got on, and the driver looked our way and said, "Let me have those seats." It did not seem proper, particularly for a woman to give her seat to a man. All the passengers paid ten cents, just as he did. When more whites boarded the bus, the driver, J.P. Blake, ordered the blacks in the fifth row, the first row of the colored section (the row I was sitting in), to move to the rear. Bus drivers then had police powers, under both municipal and state laws, to enforce racial segregation. However, we were sitting in the section designated for colored.

At first none of us moved.

"Y'all better make it light on yourselves and let me have those seats," Blake said.

Then three of the blacks in my row got up, but I stayed in my seat and slid closer to the window. I do not remember being frightened. But I sure did not believe I would "make it light" on myself by standing up. Our mistreatment was just not right, and I was tired of it. The more we gave in, the worse they treated us. I kept thinking about my mother and my grandparents, and how strong they were. I knew there was a possibility of being mistreated, but an opportunity was

Rosa Parks, who refused to surrender her bus seat to a white man, is escorted to the Montgomery, Alabama, city jail by her attorney Charles D. Langford (right), and the local deputy sheriff.

being given to me to do what I had asked of others.

I knew someone had to take the first step. So I made up my mind not to move. Blake asked me if I was going to stand up.

"No. I am not," I answered.

Blake said that he would have to call the police. I said, "Go ahead." In less than five minutes, two policemen came, and the driver pointed me out. He said that he wanted the seat and that I would not stand up.

"Why do you push us around?" I said to one of the policemen.

"I don't know," he answered, "but the law is the law and you're under arrest.'

Very Much Alone

I did not get on the bus to get arrested; I got on the bus to go home. Getting arrested was one of the worst days in my life. It was not a happy experience. Since I have always been a strong believer in God, I knew that He was with me, and only He could get me through the next step.

I had no idea that history was being made. I was just tired of giving in. Somehow, I felt that what I did was right

Hate Crimes by the Ku Klux Klan

When the Supreme Court banned segregation in the 1950s, hate groups such as the Ku Klux Klan (KKK) quickly organized to oppose integration. Members of the Klan hid their identities behind white sheets, burned crosses as a show of resistance, and incited violence throughout rural areas from North Carolina to Texas and as far north as Indiana. Members of the Klan were implicated in bombing organizations such as integrated YMCAs, churches, and synagogues. Milton Meltzer, a historian and author of over forty books, has written extensively about blacks in America, civil rights, and social change.

Millions of blacks rejoiced [over the Supreme Court's *Brown* decision] that at last—almost ninety years after Emancipation [when the Civil War ended slavery]—the basic rights of democracy for all were recognized.

But soon resistance to the Court's ruling developed. The battle for school desegregation became international news. Clinton, Nashville, Atlanta, Little Rock, Oxford—the names [of these southern towns fighting integration] flashed across the world's front pages. Refusal to comply with the law ranged from simple inaction through token integration to riots and bombings.

Only a few months after the court ruling, the White Citizens Council was born in Mississippi. The middle class organization multiplied rapidly throughout the South. It said its aim was to preserve segregation by legal means. But many councils went far beyond the bounds of the law. They turned to open and hidden terror, to economic pressure, to reprisals against whites who stood up for the law. "We intend to make it difficult, if not impossible," said a Council leader, "for any Negro who advo-

by standing up to that bus driver. I did not think about the consequences. I knew that I could have been lynched, man-handled, or beaten when the police came. I chose not to

cates desegregation to find and hold a job, get credit, or renew a mortgage."

The [Ku Klux] Klan had shrunk to a handful of chapters by the early 1950s. Now it was reborn. [Klan groups called] Klaverns sprang up all over the South like thistles after rain. They swore allegiance to any one of many self-anointed [leaders called] Wizards who declared that "his Klan and his alone was the sole surviving splinter of the true Klan cross."

Kluxers of the late Fifties went in for more than tough talk. They leaped up on the stage of the Birmingham Auditorium to attack [African American] singer Nat "King" Cole during a concert, and they organized a riot on the campus of the University of Alabama to force the trustees to expel the first black student they had admitted. They turned Clinton, Tennessee, into a raging mob town when the schools were integrated. They bombed black and white schools in many cities. In Nashville they blew a leader of the NAACP out of bed with a bomb. At the University of Mississippi they shot a newspaperman dead when James Meredith enrolled there as [the first black] student.

The toll of terrorism was staggering. In 1959 *The New York Times* reported "530 specific cases of violence, reprisal and intimidation" over the preceding four-year period in Atlanta alone. It said that resistance groups such as the KKK had spread across the South. "Gunpowder and dynamite, parades and cross burnings, anonymous telephone calls, beatings and threats have been the marks of their trade." When [African American] Mack Parker was lynched in 1959 the New York *Age* noted he was "the 578th human being in Mississippi who has met death at the hands of a mob since 1882."

Milton Meltzer, *The Truth About the Ku Klux Klan.* New York: Franklin Watts, 1982.

move. When I made that decision, I knew that I had the strength of my ancestors with me.

There were other people on the bus whom I knew. But when I was arrested, not one of them came to my defense. I felt very much alone. One man who knew me did not even go by my house to tell my husband I had been arrested. Everyone just went on their way.

In jail I felt even more alone. For a moment, as I sat in that little room with bars, before I was moved to a cell with two other women, I felt that I had been deserted. But I did not cry. I said a silent prayer and waited.

Later that evening, to my great relief, I was released. It is strange: after the arrest, I never did reach the breaking point of shedding tears. The next day, I returned to work. It was pouring down rain, so I called a cab. The young man at work was so surprised to see me. He thought I would be too nervous and shaken to go back to work.

The Beginning of the Bus Boycott

Three days later I was found guilty and ordered to pay a ten-dollar fine plus four dollars in court costs. The case was later appealed with the help of one of my attorneys, Fred Gray, and I did not have to pay anything.

It is funny to me how people came to believe that the reason that I did not move from my seat was that my feet were tired. I did not hear this until I moved to Detroit in 1957. My feet were not tired, but *I* was tired—tired of unfair treatment. I also heard later that Mother Pollard, one of the marchers in Montgomery, said that my feet were tired but my soul was rested. She was right about my soul.

On Monday, December 5, the day I went to court, the Montgomery Improvement Association (MIA) was formed to start the bus boycott. It is sad, in a way, to think about what we had to go through to get to that point. We, as a people, all felt discouraged with our situation, but we had not been united enough to conquer it. Now, the fearfulness and bitterness was turning into power.

So the people started organizing, protesting, and walking. Many thousands were willing to sacrifice the comfort and convenience of riding the bus. This was the modern mass movement we needed. I suppose they were showing sympathy for a person who had been mistreated. It was not just my arrest that year. Many African-Americans, including Emmett Till, had been killed or beaten for racist reasons. I was the third woman in Montgomery to be arrested on a bus. We reached the point where we simply had to take action.

Nearly a year later the segregated-bus ordinance was declared unconstitutional by the U.S. Supreme Court. One day after the boycott ended, I rode a nonsegregated bus for the first time.

Many Fighting for Freedom

A month after the boycott began, I lost my twenty-five-dollar-a-week job when the now-defunct Montgomery Fair department store closed its tailor shop. I was given no indication from the store that my boycott activities were the reason I lost my job. People always wanted to say it was because of my involvement in the boycott. I cannot say this is true. I do not like to form in my mind something I do not have any proof of.

Four decades later I am still uncomfortable with the credit given to me for starting the bus boycott. Many people do not know the whole truth; I would like them to know I was not the only person involved. I was just one of many who fought for freedom. And many others around me began to *want* to fight for their rights as well.

At that time, the Reverend Martin Luther King Jr. was emerging on the scene. He once said, "If you will protest courageously and yet with dignity and Christian love, when the history books are written in future generations, the historians will have to pause and say: there lived a great people—a black people—who injected new meaning and dignity into the veins of civilization." It was these words that guided many of us as we faced the trials and tribulations of fighting for our rights.

High School Integration in Little Rock

Juan Williams

By the autumn of 1957 school integration had reached Little Rock, Arkansas. The previously all-white Central High School was ordered by the federal government to admit black students. The battle had begun two years earlier when Daisy Bates, a black newspaper publisher, organized a campaign to let nine students attend Central High. Her windows were broken by a rock-throwing mob, her house was sprayed with bullets, and crosses were burned on her lawn. Forty-four teachers who favored integration were fired. As anti-integration hysteria mounted, president Dwight D. Eisenhower was forced to call in the elite 101st Airborne Division to integrate Central High. The next morning, 350 paratroopers stood in front of the school. Soldiers in jeeps mounted with machine guns took the students to school while army helicopters circled overhead.

Juan Williams has been a national correspondent for *The Washington Post*, a White House reporter, and has written for *The Atlantic, The New Republic*, and others.

The Supreme Court outlawed school segregation in its 1954 *Brown* decision, but only two southern states began desegregation that year—Texas integrated one school district;

Excerpted from *Eyes on the Prize: America's Civil Rights Years, 1954–1965*, by Juan Williams, introduction by Julian Bond. Copyright ©1987 by Blackside, Inc. Reprinted with permission from Penguin Putnam, Inc.

Arkansas, two. In the rest of the South, not a single classroom was racially mixed. Most school officials claimed they were waiting for the Supreme Court's expected implementation decision before executing an integration plan. Five of the seven states closest to the North began desegregation in 1954. But even there, acceptance of the court's ruling was slow. . . .

From the mid-forties to the mid-fifties, blacks in Little Rock made dramatic gains. Some blacks had been allowed to join the police force, and in a few neighborhoods blacks and whites lived next door to one another. In contrast to their counterparts in most southern states, thirty-three percent of all eligible Arkansas blacks were registered to vote. The library, parks, and public buses had all been integrated, and in 1955 white schools seemed ready to open their doors to blacks.

The Little Rock school board was the first in the South to issue a statement of compliance after the Supreme Court's ruling. "It is our responsibility," the board announced just five days after the decision, "to comply with federal constitutional requirements, and we intend to do so when the Supreme Court of the United States outlines the methods to be followed."

Black leaders had high hopes for a smooth transition to integrated classrooms. In the *Arkansas Gazette* and the *Arkansas Democrat,* both white-run daily newspapers, Little Rock residents read words of support for desegregation. In 1954, Daisy Bates, head of the state NAACP, called Little Rock a "liberal southern city.". . .

Governor Orval Faubus, elected in 1954, was neither a moderate nor a reactionary on race issues; he was an old-fashioned southern politician who tried to tell the people what they wanted to hear. Because the governor's term in Arkansas was only two years long, Faubus was always running for office. . . .

Choosing the Little Rock Nine

As segregationist sentiment grew during the summer, the Little Rock school board launched a quiet campaign to pare down the number of black students eligible to attend Central High School. Branton recalls, "As the summer went by and Little Rock decided that, 'Oh, my God, this thing is on us,' they started putting up all kinds of barriers. They required black children who wanted to go to white schools to register. . . . Approximately seventy-five black kids signed up to go to Central High School. And then as the opening of school approached, the Little Rock school board screened the seventy-five down to twenty-five."

Then the board tried to dissuade even those twenty-five from attending Central. According to Branton, they "began calling in parents of kids, saying, 'If you really want your son to play football, you ought to stay over there at Horace Mann [the all-black high school],' or, 'Your daughter has a magnificent voice . . . but if she goes over to the white school, and being new, she could get lost in the shuffle and won't get a chance to sing.'"

In the end, only nine black students enrolled at Central. None of the thirty-three students whose parents had sued over the slowness of the desegregation plan were among them. "The nine of the twenty-five [were] selected by the school board because they were trying to get 'good' Negroes, and none of the 'radicals' who sued them . . . ," said Branton. "They became the Little Rock Nine and carved out a place in history."

In August 1957, less than two weeks before integration was scheduled to begin, Georgia governor Marvin Griffin visited Little Rock at the invitation of the Citizens Council. He told the 300 white guests at a ten-dollar-a-plate dinner that he had no intention of complying with the Supreme Court's dictate. The only connection between the federal government and the Georgia public schools, he contended, was Uncle Sam's financial contribution to school lunches. "If they try to tell us then to integrate the races," he warned, "I will be compelled to tell them to get their black-eyed peas and soup pots out of Georgia." The crowd stood and cheered. Governor Griffin then urged them to join him in rejecting the high court's ruling. They could prevail, he

White students at Little Rock Junior High School in Little Rock, Arkansas, display their anger over the forced integration of their school. Many of Little Rock's citizens were violently opposed to the integration of the city's public schools.

said, through "the determined and cooperative efforts of a dedicated people, a steadfast general assembly and an administration committed unequivocally toward preservation of our cherished institutions . . ."

That night, a rock was thrown through Daisy Bates' living room window. "Instinctively, I threw myself to the floor," Bates later recounted in her book *The Long Shadow of Little Rock*. "I was covered with shattered glass . . . I reached for the rock lying in the middle of the floor. A note was tied to it. I broke the string and unfolded a soiled piece of paper. Scrawled in bold print were the words: 'Stone this time. Dynamite next.'". . .

Calling Up the National Guard

On September 2, the day before the schools were to open in Little Rock, Faubus went on statewide television and announced that he intended to surround Central High with National Guardsmen because of "evidence of disorder and threats of disorder."

"[This decision] has been made after conferences with dozens of people . . . ," Faubus said. "The mission of the state militia is to maintain or restore order and to protect the lives and property of citizens. They will not act as segregationists or integrationists but as soldiers . . . it will not be possible to restore or to maintain order and protect the lives and property of the citizens if forcible integration is carried out tomorrow in the schools of this community. The inevitable conclusion, therefore, must be that schools in Pulaski County, for the time being, must be operated on the same [segregated] basis as they have been operated in the past. . . ."

Daisy Bates was stunned, as was her husband, L.C. Bates, publisher of a black newspaper, the *Arkansas State Press*. "His words electrified Little Rock," Daisy Bates recounts. "By morning they shocked the United States. By noon the next day, his message horrified the world. . . . From the chair of the highest office of the state of Arkansas, Governor Orval Eugene Faubus delivered the infamous words, 'Blood will run in the streets' if Negro pupils should attempt to enter Central High School."

The next day, the first day of school, 250 National Guardsmen stood on the sidewalks outside Central High. "Little Rock arose . . . to gaze upon the incredible spectacle of an empty high school surrounded by the National Guard, troops called out by Gov. Faubus to protect life and property against a mob that never materialized," wrote the *Gazette*.

As the parents of the nine black youngsters slated to enter Central conferred with NAACP officials and lawyers, the school board issued a written statement, saying that "although the federal court has ordered integration to proceed, Governor Faubus has said that the schools should continue as they have in the past and has stationed troops at Central High to maintain order. . . .We ask that no Negro student attempt to attend Central or any white high school until this dilemma is legally resolved." The board then sought guidance from Judge Ronald Davies, the magistrate who just days earlier had ordered integration to go forward. Judge Davies immediately ordered them to proceed with the integration plan, saying that he was aware of the segregationist sentiment in Little Rock but that "I have a constitutional duty and obligation from which I shall not shrink."

Rebuffed by the court, the school board advised the nine black students to attend school the next day, September 4. Although Superintendent Blossom promised that the children would be protected, their parents were afraid. Because the board had asked the parents not to accompany their youngsters to school, explaining that the presence of the black parents might incite a mob, Daisy Bates made preparations to take the children to school. She telephoned eight sets of parents with instructions to have the children meet her at 12th Street and Park Avenue at 8:30 A.M., where two police cars would be waiting to drive them to school. But she failed to reach the Eckfords, parents of fifteen-year-old Elizabeth. They had no telephone, and Bates forgot to send a message.

As Elizabeth prepared for school the next morning, she heard the newscaster on the television wondering aloud whether the black children would dare to show up at the school. Birdee Eckford told her daughter to turn off the set. "She was so upset and worried," Elizabeth recalls. "I wanted to comfort her, so I said, 'Mother, don't worry.'" Her father paced the floor with a cigar in one hand and a pipe in the other—both unlit. The family prayed together, then Elizabeth set off for school in the crisply pressed black-and-white dress that she and her mother had made especially for this day. She walked to the public bus stop and rode off toward her new high school.

Getting off the bus near Central High, Eckford saw a throng of white people and hundreds of armed soldiers. But the presence of the guardsmen reassured her. The superintendent had told the black students to come in through the main entrance at the front of the school, so

Elizabeth headed in that direction. "I looked at all the people and thought, 'Maybe I'll be safe if I walk down the block to the front entrance behind the guards,'" she re-members. "At the corner I tried to pass through the long lines of guards around the school so as to enter the grounds behind them. One [soldier] pointed across the street . . . so

The First Day of School for Melba Beals

Melba Beals was one of the nine black students chosen to inte-grate Little Rock's Central High and the only one to show up on the first day of school. Throughout her junior year in high school she faced racists who did everything in their power to prevent her from obtaining an education. Melba Pattillo Beals earned a bach-elor's degree from San Francisco State and a graduate degree from Columbia University. She has worked as a reporter for NBC and a communications consultant.

In 1957, while most teenage girls were listening to Buddy Holly's "Peggy Sue," watching Elvis gyrate, and collecting crinoline slips, I was escaping the hanging rope of a lynch mob, dodging lighted sticks of dynamite, and washing away burning acid sprayed into my eyes.

During my junior year in high school, I lived at the center of a violent civil rights conflict. . . .

On our first day at Central High, Governor Faubus dispatched gun-toting Arkansas National Guard soldiers to prevent us from entering. Mother and I got separated from the others. The two of us narrowly escaped a rope-carrying lynch mob of men and women shouting that they they'd kill us rather than see me go to school with their children.

Three weeks later, having won a federal court order, we black children maneuvered our way past an angry mob to enter the side door of Central High. But by eleven that morning, hundreds of people outside were running wild, crashing through police barri-

I walked across the street conscious of the crowd that stood there, but they moved away from me . . . [Then] the crowd began to follow me, calling me names. I still wasn't afraid—just a little bit nervous. Then my knees started to shake all of a sudden and I wondered whether I could make it to the center entrance a block away. It was the longest

ers to get us out of school. Some of the police sent to control the mob threw down their badges and joined the rampage. But a few other brave members of the Little Rock police force saved our lives by spiriting us past the mob to safety. . . .

On my third trip to Central High, I rode with the 101st in an army station wagon guarded by jeeps with turret guns mounted on their hoods and helicopters roaring overhead. With the protection of our 101st bodyguards, we black students walked through the front door of the school and completed a full day of classes.

But I quickly learned from those who opposed integration that the soldiers' presence meant a declaration of war. Segregationists mounted a brutal campaign against us, both inside and out of school.

My eight friends and I paid for the integration of Central High with our innocence. During those years when we desperately needed approval from our peers, we were victims of the most harsh rejection imaginable. The physical and psychological punishment we endured profoundly affected all our lives. It transformed us into warriors who dared not cry even when we suffered intolerable pain.

I became an instant adult, forced to take stock of what I believed and what I was willing to sacrifice to back up my beliefs. The experience endowed me with an indestructible faith in God.

I am proud to report that the Little Rock experience also gave us courage, strength, and hope. We nine grew up to become productive citizens, with special insights about how important it is to respect the value of every human life.

Melba Pattillo Beals, *Warriors Don't Cry*. New York: Pocket Books, 1994.

block I ever walked in my whole life. Even so, I wasn't too scared, because all the time I kept thinking the [guards] would protect me.

"When I got in front of the school, I went up to a guard again," she continues. "He just looked straight ahead and didn't move to let me pass. I didn't know what to do . . . Just then the guards let some white students through . . . I walked up to the guard who had let [them] in. He too didn't move. When I tried to squeeze past him, he raised his bayonet, and then the other guards moved in and raised their bayonets. . . . Somebody started yelling, '*Lynch her! Lynch her!*'"

"A Negro Girl Is Being Mobbed"

As Daisy and L.C. Bates drove toward the appointed meeting place at 12th Street and Park Avenue, they heard a news bulletin over the car radio. "A Negro girl is being mobbed at Central High . . . ," the announcer said. L.C. jumped out of the car and ran as fast as he could to the school.

"I tried to see a friendly face somewhere in the mob . . . ," Elizabeth recalls. "I looked into the face of an old woman, and it seemed a kind face, but when I looked at her again, she spat on me."

The young woman heard someone snarl, "No nigger bitch is going to get in our school. Get out of here." The guards looked on impassively; Eckford was on her own. "I looked down the block and saw a bench at the bus stop. Then I thought, 'If I can only get there, I will be safe.'" She ran to the bench and sat down, but a cluster of ruffians had followed her. "Drag her over to the tree," said one of them, calling for a lynching.

Then Benjamin Fine, an education writer for the *New York Times,* put his arm around Elizabeth. "He raised my chin and said, 'Don't let them see you cry,'" she recalls. Finally a white woman named Grace Lorch, whose husband taught at a local black college, guided Elizabeth away from the mob. The two tried to enter a nearby drugstore to call a cab, but someone slammed the door in their faces. Then

Black students arrive under military escort at Central High School in Little Rock, Arkansas. When the police were incapable of protecting the students, President Eisenhower ordered federal troops to accompany the students to school.

they spotted a bus coming and quickly boarded it. Lorch accompanied Elizabeth home safely, but the experience had left its mark. Afterwards, the fifteen-year-old sometimes woke in the night, terrified, screaming about the mob.

The other black students did not have to face the mob alone, but they, too, failed to get past the Arkansas National Guardsmen and into Central High. . . .

People Screamed, Cursed, and Wept

On Monday morning, September 23, the Little Rock Nine gathered at Daisy Bates' home to await word from the city police on how they would get to school. Also waiting were four black journalists. The police called shortly after 8 A.M. to tell Bates they would escort the children through a side entrance of the high school, hoping to avoid the angry crowd gathering in front of the building. Bates told the reporters of the plan and advised them to drive to the school.

The black journalists arrived at Central seconds before the students. As the four got out of their car, the 8:45

school bell rang. Suddenly, someone in the throng of hundreds of whites yelled, "Look, here they come!" The reporters had apparently been mistaken for parents escorting their children to school. About twenty whites began to chase the men down the street; others soon followed. Newsman Alex Wilson chose not to flee and was savaged. "Somebody had a brick in his hand," remembers James Hicks, another of the journalists, "and instead of throwing the brick, 'cause he was too close, he hit Alex Wilson up the side of his head. . . . Wilson was more than six feet tall, an ex-Marine—he went down like a tree."

Time magazine later reported that "a cop stood on a car bumper to get a better view of the fighting. Faubus henchman James Karam [the state athletic commissioner] . . . cried angrily, 'The nigger started it.'"

Meanwhile, the three boys and six girls under police guard got out of two cars and calmly walked into the school's side entrance. "Look, they're going into the school!" someone shrieked. "Oh, my God, they're in the school!" People screamed, cursed, and wept at the sight.

With the students out of reach, the mob turned its anger on white journalists on the scene. *Life* magazine reporter Paul Welch and two photographers, Grey Villet and Francis Miller, were harassed and beaten. The photographers' equipment was smashed to the ground. The crowd began to chant to the white students now staring out of Central's windows, "Don't stay in there with them."

Before noon the mob had swelled to about a thousand people, and Police Chief Gene Smith felt compelled to quell the rioting by removing the black students from the school.

"I was in my physics class," remembers Ernest Green, the one senior among the nine black students. "A monitor came up from the principal's office [to fetch me] . . . the other eight [black students] were [in his office]. We were told by the principal that we would be sent home for our own safety. The police were having difficulty holding the mob back at the barricade, and they said if they broke through they could not be responsible for our safety." The youngsters were escorted home safely, and Daisy Bates told reporters that they would not return to Central until the president assured them they would be protected. . . .

Sending in the Paratroopers

In Washington, President Eisenhower termed the rioting a "disgraceful occurrence." Little Rock Mayor Woodrow Mann, fearing that city police could not contain the crowd if they should return the next day, called the Justice Department. He asked that the president consider sending in federal troops to enforce the court order and keep the peace at Central High. Eisenhower issued an emergency proclamation ordering all Americans to cease and desist from blocking entry to the school and obstructing the federal court order to desegregate Central.

The next morning, as Mann had expected, another restless mob of segregationists outnumbered Little Rock police at the high school. The mayor again telephoned the Justice Department. This time he formally requested the aid of federal troops.

At Eisenhower's orders, that evening more than a thousand members of the 101st Airborne Division flew to Little Rock Air Force Base from Fort Campbell, Kentucky. The Arkansas National Guard was also mobilized, but this time, they were ordered to defend the black students. . . .

That night the president went on nationwide television to explain why he was using federal troops, as the segregationists would later put it, against American citizens. "To make this talk," the president began, "I have come to the President's office in the White House. I could have spoken from Rhode Island, where I have been staying recently, but I felt that, in speaking from the house of Lincoln, of Jackson, and of Wilson, my words would better convey both the sadness I feel in the action I was compelled today to take and the firmness with which I intend to pursue this course until the orders at Little Rock can be executed without unlawful interference. In that city, under the leadership of demagogic extremists, disorderly mobs have deliberately prevented the carrying out of proper orders from a federal court. . . . This morning the mob again gathered in front of the Central High School of Little Rock, obviously for the purpose of again preventing the carrying out of the court's order relating to the admission of Negro children to that school. Whenever normal agencies prove inadequate to the task . . . the president's responsibility is inescapable . . . I have today issued an executive order directing the use of troops under federal authority to aid in the execution of federal law at Little Rock. . . . Our personal opinions about the decision have no bearing on the matter of enforcement. . . . Mob rule cannot be allowed to override the decisions of our courts. . . . [Most southerners] do not sympathize with mob rule. They, like the rest of our nation, have proved in two great wars their readiness to sacrifice for America. And the foundation of the American way of life is our national respect for law."

The federal troops surrounded Central High School. Little Rock police, who in the past few days had jailed more than forty people on charges of "inciting to riot," continued to arrest small groups of white men near the school. In the city's black neighborhoods, people were unnerved. As one news reporter later described it, "the Negro districts [were] uniformly dark and silent; where a house was lighted, the lights were switched off at the approach of the car." Police watching Daisy Bates' home followed a car that drove slowly past with its lights off. Minutes later an officer resumed to the darkened house to report that police had discovered dynamite and firearms in the vehicle.

The next morning, the Little Rock Nine again met at the Bates house, this time to be escorted to school by federal troops. . . .

"We Are Governed by Laws"

By this time, 350 paratroopers lined two blocks of Park Avenue in front of the school. Major James Meyers spoke to the gathering mob from a sound truck. "Please return to your homes or it will be necessary to disperse you," he barked. One small group called back, "Nigger lover." A man yelled, "They're just bluffing. If you don't want to move, you don't have to." Then, at the Major's order, a dozen paratroopers advanced with their bayonets poised, sending the crowd scurrying.

Inside the school, Major General Edwin A. Walker, commander of the federal forces, spoke to the white students at a special assembly. "What does all this mean to you students?" he asked. "You have often heard it said, no doubt, that the United States is a nation under law, and not under men. This means we are governed by laws . . . and not by the decrees of one man or one class of men. . . . I believe that you are well-intentioned, law-abiding citizens who understand the necessity of obeying the law. . . . You have nothing to fear from my soldiers and no one will interfere with your coming, going, or your peaceful pursuit of your studies."

The Little Rock Nine were on their way. "The convoy that went from Mrs. Bates' house to the school had a jeep in front, a jeep behind," recalls Ernest Green. "They both had machine gun mounts, [and] there were soldiers with rifles. When we got to the front of the school, the whole school was ringed with paratroopers and helicopters hovering around. We marched up the steps . . . with this circle of soldiers with bayonets drawn. . . . Walking up the steps that day was probably one of the biggest feelings I've ever had. I figured I had finally cracked it."

When the black students got inside the school, each was assigned a bodyguard. "The troops were wonderful," remembers Melba Pattillo Beals, then fifteen years old. "They were disciplined, they were attentive, they were caring, they didn't baby us, but they were there."

Eighty white students had left the school after Major General Walker addressed the assembly, but most of those remaining were very friendly to the nine newcomers. At the end of the school day, paratroopers escorted the black students back to the Bates house. One of the youngsters, Minniejean Brown, happily recounted that she had been invited by her white classmates to join the glee club. Some of the students had asked the black kids to eat lunch with them. Reporters from across the nation interviewed white children at the school. The president of the student council told reporter Mike Wallace that if only the white parents would stay away from the school, there would be no violence. Another student commented, "I think it [the opposition to integration] is downright un-American. I think it's the most terrible thing ever seen in America. I mean, I guess I'm sounding too patriotic or something, but I always thought all men were created equal."

CHAPTER 4

Suburban Culture in the Atomic Age

Moving to the Suburbs on the G.I. Bill

William L. O'Neill

According to author William L. O'Neill, Americans by and large saw the 1950s as a progressive era. The G.I. Bill, benefiting World War II veterans, focused on education and housing and stimulated a huge construction boom. Inexpensive, assembly-line housing sprang up on the East Coast, and was soon imitated everywhere. Thousands of houses, very similar in appearance and construction, crowded into instant suburbs built on the outskirts of big cities. Families could have modern appliances, individual bedrooms, garages, and lawns in the 1940s for as little as $6,000 with $99 down. Veterans used low-interest loans to snap up the houses, and the suburban boom was born.

William L. O'Neill, a professor of history at Rutgers University, is an authority on American society in the postwar period.

There were 16,354,000 Americans who served in the armed forces during World War II. Four hundred five thousand died of all causes, battle deaths being the commonest. Fewer than 100,000 more required hospitalization or other care during and immediately after the war. Most of the remainder plunged back into civilian life, the armed forces retaining only 1.5 million persons. The majority of

Excerpted from *American High: The Years of Confidence, 1945–1960,* by William L. O'Neill. Copyright ©1986 by Catherine L. O'Neill and Cassandra O'Neill. Reprinted with permission from The Free Press, a division of Simon & Schuster, Inc.

veterans were young men eager to make up for lost time. They and their wives gave the postwar era its special character, which was determined by their needs and values, the results of common experiences in war and peace. Optimistic, ambitious, hard-working, determined, they knew what they wanted and, to an impressive degree, secured it. . . . [American prosperity in the 1950s] owed more to them than to any other group.

One of the brightest things Congress ever did was to pass the Servicemen's Readjustment Act of 1944. It was taken for granted that veterans would receive some sort of extra compensation. After previous wars cash bonuses had been handed out, but this led to endless wrangling over size and times of payment. . . . After furious lobbying by the American Legion, which with 2 million members was much the largest veterans organization, the "GI Bill of Rights" was passed. Congress had decided not to hand out money in lump sums but to award it for specific purposes. The GI Bill was no bonanza. As one critic put it, "the veteran could resume his education, if he could live on $50 a month; could get the government to guarantee up to $2,000 of a loan at four percent interest to buy a house or a farm or to go into business. . . ."

College, Marriage, and a Family

Benefit levels, though never high, rose over time; but the main thing was that most veterans did qualify for aid. As a result, during its twelve years of existence, the GI Bill provided educational assistance for 7.8 million veterans, over half of those eligible. The majority were trained in technical schools or on the job; even so, 2.2 million went to colleges and universities, far more than expected and far more than would have gone had there been no GI Bill. The total spent for education and training was $14.5 billion, less than a bonus would have cost and much more valuable. Indeed, as education and training normally increased the income of recipients, and thus their tax payments, the government doubtlessly made a handsome profit on its investment. In addition the Veteran's Administration guaranteed or insured nearly $16.5 million in loans for homes, farms, and businesses. This too was a good investment that stimulated economic growth.

The GI Bill was one reason why postwar life turned out differently than had been expected. Instead of sprinkling money at random, government focused aid to veterans on

 ## William Levitt: Builder of a New Way of Life

By 1960, 60 million Americans—one-third of the population— were living in newly built suburbs that were virtually nonexistent in 1950. The chief architect of the inexpensive suburban housing development was William J. Levitt. In this excerpt, J. Ronald Oakley, a professor of history for more than two decades, writes about Levitt's method of operation.

A severe housing shortage existed at the end of the Second World War, but in the postwar period ingenious home developers rose all across the country to develop new ways of meeting the crisis in home construction—fast. Chief of these was William J. Levitt, who had originated the techniques of building standardized, low-cost housing while constructing some 2,000 units for the navy during the war. After the conflict ended, he and his sons revolutionized the housing industry by constructing entire new towns on land that had once been potato fields, pastures, or forests. Like [Ford Motor Company founder] Henry Ford, the Levitts discovered that most Americans would trade variety and style for affordability and function, so they brought the assembly-line method to housing. The land was bulldozed flat, then covered with standardized houses on standardized lots connected by standardized streets. Trees and shrubbery were systematically added after the houses had been completed. By using a uniform floor plan, seven different color choices, the same basic exterior, as many precut or prefabricated materials as possible, standard ap-

education and housing, both of which flourished to a much greater degree than after any previous war. The veterans themselves were another reason; for while traditional in some respects, they were surprisingly different in others. This was evident almost at once, though the implications took years to develop. Having spent, on the average, three years in uniform, veterans felt they had to make up for lost time.

---

pliances, and other cost-cutting techniques, the Levitts could offer a house with 721 square feet of floor space and a fully equipped kitchen for a little less than $8,000. Levittowns sprang up quickly on Long Island (with a population of 70,000 by 1953), then in New Jersey, Pennsylvania, and other parts of the country. Thousands of people who had formerly been unable to buy a house now became homeowners. Levitt and Sons made millions of dollars, and William J. Levitt, who liked to call his firm "the General Motors of the housing industry," became a national figure. On July 3, 1950, he appeared on the cover of *Time* magazine, which hailed him as the seller of "a new way of life."

Other developers knew a good thing when they saw it, and imitators of the Levitts multiplied all across the country. Thousands of new communities sprang up, complete with their own churches and schools and neighborhood recreational facilities such as swimming pools, tennis courts, and playgrounds. Almost 2 million new homes were started in 1950, and for the rest of the decade the number of new housing starts averaged around 1.5 million a year before dropping off to 1.3 million in 1960 as the housing shortage ended. Almost 25 percent of all existing homes in 1950 had been built in the previous ten years, and the number of homeowners had jumped during that decade from 23.6 million to 32.8 million. The great majority of new homes built in this time were located in the suburbs—in fact, 11 million of the 13 million new homes built between 1948 and 1958 were located in the suburbs.

J. Ronald Oakley, *God's Country: America in the Fifties.* New York: Dembner Books, 1986.

A large number enrolled in college, got married, and started a family all at once, instead of sequentially as before. . . .

Severe Housing Shortage

[A drastic housing shortage affected the veterans and new] suburbs had to be built, a massive national undertaking that started out so dismally as to give little hint of what was to come. In the early postwar years Americans, and veterans in particular, were obsessed with housing because there was so little of it. The crisis began in December 1945, according to *Life* magazine, the month when returning veterans overtaxed the housing market. They could not be absorbed because since 1932 the number of new families formed each year had exceeded the number of housing starts. Owing to depression and war there had not been a good year for residential construction since 1929. Veterans found themselves living in garages, coal sheds, cellars, even in automobiles. Chicago made 250 streetcars available for conversion into homes. A marine captain back from the Far East said it was easier to find a sniper in China than an apartment in New York. Over the next decade America would need 16.1 million new homes, declared *Life,* far more than the industry could possibly erect. Prefabrication was the only answer.

In response to the crisis President Truman appointed Wilson W. Wyatt, ex-mayor of Louisville, as his housing expediter. Wyatt was supposed to treat housing as if it were a production problem like those overcome during the war. He hoped to cut through red tape, hasten the end of supply shortages, and stimulate industrial or prefabricated housing, the favored solution to problems caused by obsolete building methods and restrictive labor practices. Wyatt called for 900,000 conventional home starts in 1947 and 600,000 prefabricated units. Over two years he hoped 2.4 million units of both types would be constructed. A *Fortune* magazine poll indicated that these were appropriate goals. [Pollster] Elmo Roper had discovered that almost 19 percent of all American families were doubled up and 19 percent were looking for a place to live. Another 13 percent would have been looking were the prospects of finding anything less grim.

By the beginning of 1947 Wyatt's program lay in ruins. There were supposed to have been 1.2 million new units constructed in 1946, but the goal was not reached owing to supply shortages. In Detroit where 100,000 units were needed only 3,000 materialized, one-seventh of the number finished in the depression year of 1939. In Seattle there were 12,000 starts and 400 completions as of November 1, 1946. . . . [In Buffalo] two out of every five married vets, some 13,000, were doubled up with friends or relatives. Yet at most perhaps 1,000 new or converted units would be added to Buffalo's housing supply.

Further, the new units were not only scarce but expensive. It was estimated that a veteran would need to earn $58 a week to buy the average house, but the average weekly income of Buffalo vets was only $46. . . .

Building Levittowns

Yet the housing shortage disappeared anyway. The GI Bill was one reason; by guaranteeing loans for veterans, it assured builders of a mass market. Over a million veterans had received home loans by the end of 1947. Builders, in turn, learned to erect conventional housing on an enormous scale at reasonable prices, something that at first seemed impossible. Foremost among these heroes was William Levitt. With his brother Alfred he owned a family construction firm, Levitt and Sons. At the end of World War II they bought 1200 acres of farm land on Long Island and were soon finishing a house every fifteen minutes. These were four room expandable [Cape Cod–style homes], not cracker boxes, yet they sold for thousands less than other builders charged for similar housing. The Levitts achieved this miracle by building and buying in volume. Levitt crews poured concrete slabs and were followed by other crews who assembled houses out of materials that had been, to a large extent, precut in Levitt shops. The lumber came from Levitt

141

mills, and much of the hardware came from Levitt factories. Levitt employees were not unionized, eliminating restrictive work rules. Building in a rural area freed the Levitts from many obsolete codes. In 1950 Levittown had 10,600 houses (ultimately there would be 17,447) and was home to over 40,000 people. An entire community the size of Pough-keepsie had been created by one company in less than five years. *Time* magazine failed to name William Levitt as its man of the year, a regrettable oversight, though it did put him on the cover once. Few deserved the honor more.

Other builders followed suit. In 1947 Los Angeles, with about 2.5 percent of the nation's population, was getting 9 percent of all new housing. Climate had something to do with this, economies of scale even more. Of 60,000 houses and rental units built in Los Angeles in 1947 two-thirds were erected by only sixty builders. The ten largest put up an average of 1,400 single family dwellings each. They too used standardized plans, precut lumber, and gangs of workers. . . .

Leaving the Poor Behind

A social price was paid for [this suburbanization of America] however. Most new housing was built in suburban areas that nonwhites were barred from, kept out by low incomes, racial prejudice, or—usually—both. Blacks migrating north by the millions were forced into deteriorated central cities abandoned by the new suburbanites. People recognized that this was happening at the time, census figures later confirming their impression. In 1950 the suburban population was 20,872,000, of whom fewer than a million were nonwhite. In 1960 the white suburban population had grown by about 16 million, while there were only about 800,000 more suburban nonwhites. In central cities during this same period the population grew, in round numbers, from 48.4 million to 57.8 million, with whites accounting for about 5.5 million of the increase and nonwhites 3.9 million. This meant that in metropolitan areas white population growth was largely suburban while black growth was largely urban—and inner-city urban at that.

Teen Time in America

J. Ronald Oakley

By the mid-1950s, post–World War II baby boomers were turning into teenagers, the first generation raised on television, rock music, and economic affluence. Until the fifties, teenagers were not generally recognized as a separate demographic group. In earlier years—especially during the depression—the majority of teens left school as early as age fourteen and went directly to work. At that point they were popularly, though not legally, thought of as adults.

The growing economy of the fifties changed this perception, and teens were suddenly viewed as powerful consumers pursuing their own version of postwar prosperity—and changing American culture while they did it.

J. Ronald Oakley, author of several books, has taught college-level American and world history for over twenty years.

As the 1950s opened, America's adolescents were basically a conservative, unrebellious lot. Although the word *teenager* had come into widespread circulation in the 1940s to describe this distinct age group mired in the limbo between puberty and adulthood, the teenagers of the early fifties had not yet developed a distinct subculture. They had few rights and little money of their own, wore basically the same kind of clothing their parents wore, watched the same television shows, went to the same movies, used the same slang, and listened to the same romantic music sung by Perry Como, Frank Sinatra, and other middle-aged or nearly middle-aged artists. Their idols were . . . prominent members of the older generation. In spite of what they learned from older kids and from the underground pornography that circulated on school playgrounds, they were amazingly naive about sex, believing well into their high school years that French kissing could cause pregnancy or that the douche, coitus interruptus, and chance could effectively prevent it. Heavy petting was the limit for most couples, and for those who went "all the way" there were often strong guilt feelings and, for the girl at least, the risk of a bad reputation. Rebellion against authority, insofar as it occurred, consisted primarily of harmless pranks against unpopular adult neighbors or teachers, occasional vandalism (especially on Halloween night), smoking cigarettes or drinking beer, and the decades-old practice of mooning. Although most families had the inevitable clashes of opinion between parents and offspring, there were few signs of a "generation gap" or of rebellion against the conventions of the adult world.

Stirrings of Rebellious Behavior

But all of this began to change in the early fifties, and by the middle of the decade the appearance of a distinct youth subculture was causing parents and the media to agonize over the scandalous behavior and rebellious nature of the nation's young people. The causes of the emergence of this subculture are not hard to find. One was the demographic revolution of the postwar years that was increasing the influence of the young by producing so many of them in such a short period of time. Another was the affluence of the period, an affluence shared with the young through allowances from their parents or through part-time jobs. As teenagers acquired their own money, they were able to pursue their own life-style, and now American business and advertisers geared up to promote and exploit a gigantic youth consumer market featuring products designed especially for them. Then there were the effects of progressive education and . . . child-rearing practices, for while neither was quite as permissive or indulgent toward the young as the critics claimed, they did emphasize the treatment of adolescents as unique people who should be given the freedom to develop their own personality and talents. Another factor was television and movies, which had the power to raise up new fads, new heroes, and new values and to spread them to young people from New York to Los Angeles. And finally, there was rock 'n' roll, which grew from several strains in American music and emerged at mid-decade as the theme song of the youth rebellion and as a major molder and reflector of their values. . . .

Rowdyism, Riot, and Revolt

Another sign of the changes occurring in the nation's youth was the rise of juvenile delinquency. Between 1948 and 1953 the number of juveniles brought into court and charged with crimes increased by 45 percent, and it was estimated that for every juvenile criminal brought into court there were at least five who had not been caught. It was especially disturbing that juvenile crimes were committed by organized gangs that roamed—and seemed to control—the streets of many of the larger cities. Street gangs had existed before in American history, but in the fifties they were larger, more violent, and more widespread than ever before. Thanks to modern communications, they tended to dress alike, to use the same jargon, and share the same values all across the country And they were not just in America—they appeared in England (Teddy Boys), Sweden ("Skinn-Nuttar" or leather jackets), and other industrial countries across the globe. The youth rebellion, including the criminal fringe that made up part of it, was international.

Learning about these gangs in their newspapers and weekly magazines, Americans were horrified by what they read and by how often they read it. It seemed that hardly a week went by without the occurrence of shocking crimes committed by teenagers or even younger children who did not seem to know the difference between good and bad—or worse, deliberately chose the bad over the good. Sporting colorful names like Dragons, Cobras, Rovers, and Jesters, they carried all kinds of weapons—zip guns, pistols, rifles, knives, chains, shotguns, brass knuckles, broken bottles, razors, lead pipes, molotov cocktails, machetes, and lye and other chemicals. They drank alcoholic beverages, smoked reefers, took heroin and other drugs, had their own twisted code of honor, and organized well-planned attacks on other gangs or innocent victims. They also had their own jargon, borrowed from the criminal underworld and spoken by gangs from coast to coast: *dig, duke, gig, jap, jazz, rumble, turf, cool, chick, pusher, reefer,* and hundreds of other slang terms.

To a nation accustomed to believing in the essential goodness of its young people, the behavior of these delinquent gangs was puzzling and frightening. They seemed to pursue violence for the pure joy of violence and to delight in sadistic actions toward other gangs or innocent victims. They engaged in shootings, stabbings, individual and gang rapes, senseless beatings, and unspeakable tortures. They extorted "protection" money from frightened merchants, sprayed crowds in streets or restaurants or subways with rifle fire, doused people with gasoline and set them ablaze, firebombed bars and nightclubs, stole automobiles, vandalized apartments and public buildings, and fought vicious gang wars over girls or invasion of turf or to avenge some real or imagined slight. They often terrorized and vandalized schools and assaulted teachers and students, leading the *New York Daily News* in 1954 to describe "rowdyism, riot, and revolt," as the new three Rs in New York's public schools.

It was particularly disturbing that these young hoodlums often showed no remorse for their actions, recounting with delight to police or social workers the details of a rape, murder, or torture in which they had been involved. . . .

Hip Cat Fashion

In addition to obtaining their own music, movies, television shows, and idols, teenagers of the fifties also acquired their own fashions, and here they followed the trend toward casual dress that was characterizing the rest of society. The favorite dress of high school boys was denim jeans with rolled-up cuffs, sport shirts, baggy pegged pants, pleated rogue trousers with a white side stripe, slacks with buckles in the back, V-neck sweaters, buttondown striped shirts, blazers, white bucks, and loafers. In 1955 they also joined older males on college campuses and executive offices in the pink revolution, donning pink shirts, pink striped or polka dot ties, and colonel string ties. Hair styles ranged from the popular flat top or crew cut to the Apache or ducktail (banned at some high schools). "Greasers" of course shunned the Ivy League and pink attire as too effeminate, sticking to their T-shirts (often with sleeves rolled up to hold a cigarette pack), jeans, leather jackets, and ducktails. For girls, the fashions ranged from rolled-up jeans to casual blouses or men's shirts, full dresses with crinolines, skirts and sweaters, blazers, occasional experiments with the tube dress and sack dress and other disasters foisted upon older women by fashion designers, short shorts (with rolled-up cuffs) that got progressively shorter as the decade wore on, two-piece bathing suits (few were bold enough to wear the bikini, imported from France in the late forties), brown and white saddle shoes and loafers, and hair styles from the poodle to the ponytail. Couples who were going steady wore one another's class rings, identification tags, and necklaces or bracelets, and often adopted a unisex look by wearing matching sweaters, blazers, and shirts.

Like the generations before them, the teenagers of the fifties also had their slang. Much of it was concerned, of course, with the great passion of teens, cars. Cars were *wheels,* tires were *skins,* racing from a standing start was called a *drag,* the bumper was the *nerf-bar,* a special kind of exhaust system was called *duals,* and a car specially modified for more engine power was a *hot rod* or *souped up car* or *bomb*. A drive-in movie was a *passion pit*, anything or anyone considered dull was a *drag*, and a really dull person was a *square* or a *nose-bleed*. An admirable or poised individual or anything worthy of admiration or approval was *cool* or *neat* or *smooth*, someone who panicked or lost his *cool* was accused of *clutching*, and people admonished not to worry were told to *hang loose*. Teenagers also borrowed lingo from the jazz and beatnik world, such as *dig, hip, cat, bread,* and *chick*. A cutting, sarcastic laugh at someone's bad joke was expressed by *a hardeeharhar*. And teenagers also shared the jargon of the rest of society—*big deal, the royal screw* or *royal shaft, up the creek without a paddle, forty lashes with a wet noodle, wild, wicked, crazy, classy, horny, . . . looking for action, bad news, out to lunch, gross, fink, loser, creep, dumb cluck, doing the deed, going all the way,* or *coming across*. Many of these colloquialisms were borrowed from earlier generations, sometimes with modifications in meaning, while some had been region-

The automobile gave teenagers in the 1950s a greater feeling of independence than any generation before it.

alisms that now became national through the great homogenizing power of television.

So Much Money

By the mid-1950s there were 16.5 million teenagers in the United States. About half of them were crowding the nation's secondary schools, while the rest had entered college or the work world. Wherever they were, they had become, as Gereon Zimmerman would write in *Look* magazine, a "Generation in a Searchlight," a constant subject of media attention and a constant source of anxiety for their parents and the rest of the adult world. As Zimmerman observed, "No other generation has had so much attention, so much admonition, so many statistics."

Zimmerman might also have added that no other young generation had had so much money. One of the most revolutionary aspects of the teenage generation was its effects on the American economy, for by the midfifties teenagers made up a very lucrative consumer market for American manufacturers. By mid-decade teenagers of this affluent era were viewing as necessities goods that their parents, reared during the depression, still saw as luxuries, such as automobiles, televisions, record players, cameras, and the like. By the midfifties, teenagers were buying 43 percent of all records, 44 percent of all cameras, 39 percent of all new radios, 9 percent of all new cars, and 53 percent of movie tickets. By 1959, the amount of money spent on teenagers by themselves and by their parents had reached the staggering total of $10 billion a year. Teenagers were spending around $75 million annually on single popular records, $40 million on lipstick, $25 million on deodorant, $9 million on home permanents, and over $837 million on school clothes for teenage girls. Many teenagers had their own charge accounts at local stores and charge cards issued especially for them, such as Starlet Charge Account, Campus Deb Account, and the 14 to 21 Club. Like their parents, teenagers were being led by the affluence and advertising of the age to desire an ever-increasing diet of consumer goods and services and to buy them even if they had to charge them against future earnings.

Many adults had a distorted image of this affluent young generation, focusing too much on its delinquency, rock 'n' roll, unconventional hair styles and clothing, and dating and sexual practices. Only a very small percentage were delinquents or problem-ridden adolescents. Most were reasonably well-groomed, well-behaved, and active in school and extracurricular functions. Most were interested in sports, automobiles, movies, rock 'n' roll, dating, dancing, hobbies, radio, and television. Their major worries were the typical problems of youth in an affluent age: problems with their parents, their popularity with other teens, their looks and complexions, proper dating behavior, sex, first dates, first kisses, love, bad breath, body odors, posture, body build, friends, schoolwork, college, future careers, money, religion, and the draft.

These teenagers that parents worried so much about were remarkably conservative. Survey after survey of young people in the fifties found that over half of them— and sometimes even larger percentages—believed that censorship of printed materials and movies was justified, that politics was beyond their understanding and was just a dirty game, that most people did not have the ability to make important decisions about what was good for them, that masturbation was shameful and perhaps harmful, that women should not hold public office, and that the theory of evolution was suspect and even dangerous. Like their parents, they were also very religious as a group, tending to believe in the divine inspiration of the Bible, heaven and hell, and a God who answered the prayers of the faithful. They were suspicious of radical groups and were willing to deny them the right to assemble in meetings and to disseminate their ideas, and they saw nothing wrong with denying accused criminals basic constitutional rights, such as the right to know their accuser, to be free from unreasonable search or seizure of their property, or to refuse to testify against themselves. Teenagers were also very conformist: They were very concerned about what their friends thought of their dress, behavior, and ideas, and they tried very hard to be part of the group and not be labeled an oddball or individualist. In short, in this age of corporation man, the country also had corporation teen.

Most teens were also conservative in their approach to dating, sex, and marriage. Religious views, social and peer pressure, and fear of pregnancy all combined to create this conservatism and to ensure that most teens kept their virginity until marriage or at least until the early college years, though heavy petting was certainly prevalent among couples who were engaged or "going steady," a practice reflecting society's emphasis on monogamy. These conservative attitudes toward sexual behavior were reinforced by the authorities teenagers looked to for guidance—parents, teachers, ministers, advice to the lovelorn columnists like Dear Abby and Ann Landers (both of whom began their columns in the midfifties), and books on teenage etiquette by Allen Ludden, Pat Boone, and *Seventeen* magazine. In his book for young men, *Plain Talk for Men Under 21*, Ludden devoted an entire chapter to such things as "That Good Night Kiss"—discussing whether to, how to, and the significance of it if you did. And in the very popular *The Seventeen Book of Young Living* (1957), Enid Haupt, the editor and publisher of *Seventeen* magazine, advised young girls to "keep your first and all your romances on a beyond reproach level" and to save themselves for the one right man in their lives. Acknowledging that "it isn't easy to say no to a persuasive and charming boy," she offered one answer for all potentially compromising situations: "'No, please take me home. Now.'". . .

Coming Generation Gap

By the late fifties America's teenagers had acquired a distinct subculture of their own. They had their own money, music, movies, television shows, idols, clothing, and slang. In contrast to previous generations, they were more affluent, better educated, talked more openly about sex, had greater mobility through the widespread ownership of automobiles by their parents or themselves, demanded and received more personal freedom, had more conflicts with their parents, and were the subject of more media and parental concern. But they were not yet in rebellion, for although their life-style had departed from the conventions of their elders, their basic ideas and attitudes were still the conservative ones that mirrored the conservatism of the affluent age in which they grew up.

Still, their parents were worried. As *Look* magazine reported in 1958 in an article entitled "What Parents Say About Teenagers," "many parents are in a state of confusion or despair about their teenagers. And they don't exactly know what to do about it. They would like to sit down with their children and talk over their mutual problems, but often this desire is thwarted by the teenagers themselves." The much-heralded generation gap was coming into view. In the next decade, when the junior high and senior high school students of the fifties crowded the colleges, marched in civil rights demonstrations, protested the Vietnam War, and engaged in unconventional sexual and drug practices, it would take on the temper of a revolution.

"Fitting In" for Fifties Women

Brett Harvey

During World War II, with millions of men off fighting, women were suddenly freed of traditional roles in society. For the first time, large numbers of women worked in heavy industry, drove streetcars, flew airplanes, played in orchestras, and even played on national baseball teams. After the war, women were expected to give up their jobs, marry returning soldiers, and raise families. Women who did not marry, who worked outside the home, or who did not have children were considered odd. Women who bore children out of wedlock were ostracized.

According to journalist Brett Harvey, whose work has appeared in the *Village Voice, Mother Jones, Mirabella, Ms.,* and the *New York Times Book Review,* before the feminist movement, 1950s women were second-class citizens whose roles were utterly restricted by business, the media, and by social pressures.

"**D**id you ever think about the fact that all the fabrics we wore in the fifties were *stiff?*" my friend Ronnie once asked me. I hadn't, but the minute she said it I thought: faille, shantung, felt, taffeta, pique. Nothing clung, or fell, or draped—everything was crisp.

Forties clothes were truly sexy—those swingy little dresses in soft, flowered rayon prints with shoulder pads

---

had a jaunty, competent femininity. Fifties clothes were like armor. Our clothes expressed all the contradictions of our roles. Our ridiculously starched skirts and hobbling sheaths were a caricature of femininity. Our cinched waists and aggressively pointed breasts advertised our availability at the same time they warned of our impregnability.

In the daytime we wore tight, revealing sweaters, but they were topped by mincing little Peter Pan collars and perky scarves that seemed to say, "Who, *me?* Why, I'm just a little girl!" At night our shoulders were naked, our breasts half-bare, the lower half of our bodies hidden in layers of tulle. Underneath it all, our flesh, like our volatile sexuality, was "contained" by boned girdles and Merry Widows, in an era when "containment" was a political as well as a social obsession.

Americans have a kind of fondness for the fifties. We think of it as a jokey, cartoonish decade, full of too-bright colors, goofy space-age designs, outlandish people and events, extreme ideas. We collect streamlined appliances, big-finned cars, poodle skirts and Hula Hoops as artifacts from an exotic and slightly ridiculous era. We pore over *Life* magazines of the period, enthralled by the crisp black-and-white photos of couples in bomb shelters, the ads in which smiling, wholesome teenagers toss back Cokes, and families speed down country roads in gigantic Chryslers with Dad at the wheel. Behind our bemused fascination lies a yearning for a past as black-and-white as those old *Life* photographs. Under our nervous, condescending laughter at the old "Father Knows Best" episodes lies a longing for a time when women were women, men were men, and the rules were clear.

What some of us tend to forget—and what many of us are too young to remember—is that the engine that drove the rules was fear.

Shaped by Depression and War

There was much to be afraid of in the postwar era, or so we thought. An American girl who was fifteen years old on

VJ Day in 1946 had experienced two profoundly disturbing events. Her childhood had almost certainly been touched, if not severely disrupted, by the Depression. Her father might have lost his job, her mother gone back to work. Her family might have been split up and she and her siblings separated, farmed out to relatives.

World War II created new kinds of instability. Fathers, uncles, friends, and fiancés vanished, some never to come back. In spite of more jobs, higher wartime earnings, and an easing of certain kinds of hardships, a sense of deprivation and scarcity persisted. Rubber and gasoline shortages meant you couldn't travel far from home. Public transportation was congested, housing was scarce, schools were overcrowded. Meat, butter, sugar, and many other things were rationed. Blackouts, air raids, warning sirens in the night, first aid courses in how to bandage the wounded, and, more than anything else, newsreels showing ruined cities, exploding buildings, endless lines of haunted-looking people trudging down muddy roads with their suitcases on their backs—these things created fear, uneasiness, a sense of vulnerability.

And though America had emerged from the war a major power, the world itself appeared more dangerous than ever. We had an enemy, Russia, who not only had an A-bomb, but powerful missiles aimed straight at us. The "Red tide" of Euro-Communism was headed our way as well, our leaders warned us, an evil force whose goal was nothing less than the destruction of "our American way of life." This fear of the enemy outside was easily manipulated by demagogues like Senator Joe McCarthy into a suspicion of subversion within, which rapidly spread into a queasy fear of difference itself. . . .

For women, the postwar era represented a dramatic retreat from the trends of previous decades. From the twenties through World War II, women had been steadily expanding their sphere by going to college and going to work in growing numbers. The war years brought huge numbers of women into the work force doing jobs that had been previously open only to men. It was a turbulent time when everyone's life seemed to change practically overnight. Thousands of people left home, migrating to urban areas. Not only were women making money, but many were living alone or with other women, many experiencing independence and self-sufficiency for the first time. The rigid sexual codes of previous times rapidly gave way to a more free-and-easy sexuality. Even the movies of the thirties and early forties glamorized the image of the plucky, resourceful career gal, epitomized by Rosalind Russell in *His Girl Friday* (1940).

When the war was over, all these changes raised worrisome questions among government leaders and social scientists. What if women had come to enjoy their independence and didn't want to give up their jobs to returning veterans? What if women's sexuality couldn't be curbed? What if not enough of them were willing to return home and start creating the nuclear families that would in turn create the demand for goods that the nation's prosperity depended on?

Inducements to Early Marriage

The response of government, aided by the social scientists and the media, was a massive effort to channel all these disturbing energies into one safe harbor: the family. In *Homeward Bound: American Families in the Cold War Era*, Elaine Tyler May explains that the home was the perfect vehicle for domestic containment: "Within its walls potentially dangerous social forces of the new age might be tamed, where they could contribute to the secure and fulfilling life to which postwar women and men aspired. . . . More than merely a metaphor for the cold war on the homefront, containment aptly describes the way in which public policy, personal behavior, and even political values were focused on the home."

A young woman approaching adulthood after the war was surrounded by powerful inducements to early marriage. The whole country seemed full of young men eager to date, to marry, to get on with their lives. They were glamorous, these returning soldiers. They'd been through something; they'd seen the world; they were sexually experienced; they were practically irresistible.

Magazines and newsreels were full of beaming couples buying homes, appliances, and shiny new cars. By 1956 Americans were buying 20,000 television sets a day and two out of every three families owned at least one set. Night after night, situation comedies like "Father Knows Best" and "Ozzie and Harriet," television dramas and commercials, drove home their powerful messages about male and female identity, their blueprint for family life.

Insecurity and Self-Doubt

As women, we were constantly warned about dangers, many of them hidden. The advertising industry taught us about the germs, odors, and wetness, insidious and often invisible, that could sabotage our confidence and make us unlovable. We learned we needed to be "extra-careful" about "personal hygiene," and that vaginal odor was "a grave womanly offense." We knew bad breath could make the difference between "laughter and love and marriage almost before you know it" and "boredom and loneliness."

"Insecurity" and "self-doubt" were our buzzwords. We worried about not being clean enough, or womanly enough, about not finding husbands, about not being good enough mothers. We were afraid of "getting a reputation," of "being a cock-tease," and we were terrified of getting pregnant. We made our life decisions on the basis of safety and security. We chose solid, reliable mates and valued maturity above all other personal qualities.

Increasingly, marriage and family were expected to be a woman's whole world. Her intelligence, energy, creativity, and sexuality all were funneled into the constricted sphere of family life. This narrowing of women's sphere was reinforced by the lack of desirable options outside of marriage. The professions, except for nursing and teaching, were virtually closed to women, and most of the jobs available to them were dead-end and poorly paid. Sexual experience was difficult to come by and risky unless you were married. Sexual activity could result in the loss of reputation—an essential commodity if marriage was to be your sole identity. More important, in the absence of legal abortion, an extramarital pregnancy could be—and almost always was—disastrous.

V-8 Powered Chariots of Fire

Karal Ann Marling

According to Karal Ann Marling, automobiles of the 1940s were distinctly rounded, humped, and ponderous. But the rockets and airplanes of World War II inspired 1950s automakers to build flashy cars with wraparound windshields, vast expanses of chrome, V-8 engines, and pointy tail fins crowned with giant red taillights. The interiors were loaded with new options such as radios, air conditioners, padded dashboards, and elegant upholstery. The American public was mesmerized.

As Detroit automakers set new production records each year, America's love of the automobile changed everything from rock-and-roll lyrics to where people lived.

Karal Ann Marling is professor of Art History and American studies at the University of Minnesota in Minneapolis and coauthor of two books about World War II.

There's something wonderful, disquieting, and, in the end, embarrassing about America's automobiles of the 1950s: the lunkers, the dreamboats, the befinned, bechromed behemoths that lurked in the driveways of several million brand new ranch houses in the suburbs (because they wouldn't fit in the garage!). They were the kinds of cars, those bloated GMs, Fords, and Chryslers, that Danny Thomas and Ozzie and Harriet drove on TV. . . .

They were the kind of car that Ward Cleaver, "The Beaver's" sagacious Dad, parked every week at the curb in front of 211 Pine Street, Mayfield, USA (a suburb of Utopia). The situation comedies were always set in mythical places like Mayfield, part small town, part exotic postwar California subdivision. Perpetually sunny, easy and perfect, the new West Coast way of life soon became the American ideal. The people who lived there apparently thought nothing of driving twenty miles for a routine afternoon of shopping, either. "Their enormous automotive mobility and the decentralization of their shops and playgrounds have tended to make conventional city life obsolete," said *Life* of the trendsetting Californians on whom the TV families were based. And in prime time, the nation aspired to the condition of these golden, godlike creatures in their insolent chariots. . . .

Two-Car Families

It was the urbanist Lewis Mumford, addressing an international congress of city planners in 1957, who derided big American automobiles as killers—"fantastic and insolent chariots," he termed them—and predicted that "either the motor car will drive us all out of the cities or the cities will have to drive out the motor car." By 1957, however, the American family had already piled into the car and headed for Levittown or Southern California. Desi, Lucy, and the Mertzes from the apartment upstairs drove out to Hollywood during the 1954–55 TV season, and in 1956 *I Love Lucy* moved to Connecticut for the duration. Desi became a commuter; the Ricardo family built a barbecue, met the neighbors, and hobnobbed at the Country Club. Perhaps they were lured away from town by advertising that wrapped up family life, suburbia, and new cars in one neat and appealing package. A 1956 Chevrolet campaign made the case for the two-car family with a scene showing a barbecue in progress on an expansive lawn out in front of a double carport somewhere in exurban America: "Going our separate ways we've never been so close! The family with two cars gets twice as many chores completed, so there's more leisure to enjoy *together*." General Motors, the company that made the Chevies, was the biggest advertiser of the decade. In 1955 alone, GM spent $162 million to persuade viewers, would-be suburbanites, and the rest of the nation to buy its cars. And in 1956 GM led the Top Ten Advertisers list again, nosing out Ford (number three) and Chrysler (a distant seventh).

Influencing Russian Spies

The GMs, Fords, and Chryslers of the 50s were the kinds of cars that drove foreigners to exasperated outbursts of envy, so baroque and, well, so *American* did they seem in their excesses of horsepower and gadgetry. Detroit had lobbied hard for passage of the Interstate Highway Act of 1956, but from the other side of the Atlantic the logic of building huge cars to fill up the freeways created to accommodate a growing volume of same seemed a little strained. In the tighter spaces of a Europe in the throes of persistent postwar shortages, the design critic Reyner Banham recalled, American cars looked "like space ships, or visitors from another planet or something." The intake scoop on the 1951 Cadillac was the supreme insult: the Caddy was *air conditioned* at a time when perhaps five buildings in the whole of Britain possessed such amenities. The design historian Bevis Hillier goes so far as to claim that [two] English spies . . . were driven mad by [Detroit's cars], that they were propelled into the austere embrace of the Soviet KGB by the sheer garishness of the two-tone [American] family cruiser with 285 horses under the hood. As Europe lay in ruins, the Yanks (who owned three-fourths of all the cars in the world) indulged themselves in a veritable orgy of Naugahyde and power steering. . . . Any decent chap might turn to espionage under such provocation. "Whilst the Russians had been developing 'Sputnik,'" wrote a disgusted Banham . . . , "the Americans had been debauching themselves with tailfins."

The 1958 model year that followed the launch of Sputnik was a disaster for the U.S. automotive industry. New-car sales dipped to their lowest levels since 1948. The Edsel bombed. The economy slid into a recession. Ike's ad men tried to persuade consumers to step on the gas: "You Auto Buy!" was the official slogan of the government's psychological offensive against unpatriotic, stay-at-home thrift.

 ## The Invasion of the Beetle

The culture of the gigantic, gas-guzzling automobile took a significant step forward in the 1950s, as car ownership became an indispensable fact of life for most Americans. By the late 1950s, however, an economic recession caused millions of Americans to forsake the chrome-laden Detroit monstrosities for the Volkswagen Beetle and other compact cars. Veteran newspaper reporter Rob Leicester Wagner is a regular contributor to several automotive publications as well as the author of three books about cars.

For the first time in the twentieth century, Americans [of the 1950s] had significant disposable income. One-sixth of all personal income in the average family was spent on leisure. Time away from work and the home was of paramount concern to suburban families. Auto advertisers tapped into this, particularly in the print media, with an emphasis on beautiful locales to sell cars. Splashy color advertisements displayed families in their four-door Studebaker Champions or Commanders at the beach or on a rural road to fun and sunshine. Golf courses provided the backdrop for Mercury, and the beach or waterfront for Ford and Chevrolet. Even casual sportswear, with plaids, loud colors, and loosely fitted shirts and shorts, offered a break from the rigid hierarchy of nine-to-five jobs and colorless homes.

Leisure time . . . meant travel. The Eisenhower administration implemented the National Defense Highway Act of 1956 to develop a 41,000-mile interstate highway system. This led indirectly to a mini economic boom that spawned hundreds of new

The White House seemed unsure as to whether the recession had hurt the car business or vice versa. But the Russian Sputnik made everybody queasy about fiddling with annual model changes, color charts, and cosmetic engineering while the enemy was investing in serious rocketry. The contrast was all the more pointed in that the space

motels, garages, new and used car dealers, and drive-ins of various types. New surges in rubber and petroleum consumption helped fuel the economy. Receipts in 1958 from the nation's 56,000 motels totaled $850 million. It was all evidence that Americans, desperate to leave work and home behind, were traveling in unprecedented numbers.

The chromed and finned automobile in this feel-good era symbolized, even for the briefest of moments, the independence of American workers. . . .

When the 1958 recession hit [however], the buying public began to lose patience. By the summer of 1958 unemployment had hit 7.7 percent, the highest since 1941. The old order in the automotive industry was gone.

The final blow came with a bug that would infect car owners for generations to come. Volkswagen, which rose from the ashes of a bombed out Germany in 1945, had sold nearly 200,000 Beetles by 1957. This signaled the public's rejection of Detroit's offerings. By 1959, Studebaker debuted its compact Lark; GM offered the Corvair, and Ford presented the Falcon in 1960—and no one in Detroit or in Studebaker's South Bend, Indiana plant liked it one bit. GM brass, in fact, hated the Corvair so much that they were surprised, and even disappointed, that the little car offered so much room inside. Perhaps in an act of spite, they ordered the roofline lowered to sacrifice headroom and comfort. Nevertheless, Corvair sales revived the industry and heralded a new era.

Rob Leicester Wagner, *Fabulous Fins of the Fifties*. New York: MetroBooks, 1997.

rocket had been one of the most prominent motifs attached to the car by advertising. The Olds 88, for instance, was the "Rocket 88," always paired pictorially with a sleek missile zooming skyward overhead. In the early 50s, the car itself still had a dowdy streamlined shape, all curves and bulges, despite a bumper that resembled the intake duct of a jet-interceptor. But the "Futuramic" engine under the hood went from 135 horsepower in 1951 to 202 (a takeoff speed of 110 miles per hour) in 1955: the Olds fed a growing appetite for speed and performed like a rocket long before it actually looked like one.

Rock 'n' Roll and the Olds "Rocket 88"

One memorable advertisement for the Olds 88 even put Mr. and Mrs. America, hats and purses and all, astride a moon rocket, cartoon style. It wasn't entirely serious. Speed, rocket ships, and their interstellar passengers took on an aura of fantasy and fun. And there's a greedy innocence about the pleasure cars *cum* rockets brought to the postwar United States, too, an innocence wasted on censorious English design critics. Rock 'n' roll lyrics caught the mood best, as in Jackie Brenston's "Rocket 88" of 1951 (an R&B song well on its way to rock) and Chuck Berry's 1955 hymn to speed and freedom and the thrill of the chase:

> As I was motivatin' over the hill
> I saw Maybellene in a Coup de Ville;
> A Cadillac a-rollin' on the open road,
> Nothin' will outrun my V-8 Ford.

Berry was pursuing Maybellene down the highway of desire in an old Ford. Behind the wheel of a 1955 Ford, so the catchphrase went, "you become a new man." Buick ads—Buicks were often shown gliding among the planets like garish spacecraft—also strove to attach masculinity and sexual prowess to horsepower. Driving a new Buick, read one memorable line of copy, "makes you feel like the man you are." John Keats, who made a career out of savaging automotive hype in the 1950s, dismissed the wording as "just

Buicks, Oldsmobiles, and Pontiacs roll off the assembly line in 1955.
Americans' higher incomes led to an increased demand for new cars.

another way of saying we can't distinguish between illusion
and reality, but that buying a Buick will create . . . the *illu-*
sion that we *really are* what we *really are*." But a Ford, an
Olds, or a Buick was as much daydream as no-money-

down, easy-credit-terms dreamboat. If the cars were complex beyond all telling with their Dynaflow pushbutton transmissions, their power brakes, automatic windows, vacuum ashtrays, retractable roofs, and wraparound windshields, the feelings they aroused in driver/owners were straightforward: after the privations of the Depression, after the hardships and the shortages of a war with no new models, victorious Americans deserved nothing but the best.

Within a year of the Japanese surrender, 12 million G.I.s had been sent home, every last one of them in search of a girl, a car, a new house. . . . In 1945, 70,000 cars rolled off the assembly line; in 1950, 6,665,000. Between 1945 and 1955, the number of registered motor vehicles doubled; in 1955, Detroit shipped 8,000,000 new automobiles to showrooms. The good life rolled by on big, soft Goodyear tires. It was the car that fueled the new industrial prosperity, created the suburbs where new houses sprouted like dandelions after rain, and shaped the suburban lifestyle whose manners and mores were codified in the TV sitcoms of the 1950s. The car was the new Conestoga wagon on the frontier of consumerism, a powerful instrument of change, a chariot of fiery desire. . . .

As the design historian Thomas Hine has suggested, the doctrine of luxury for all—what he calls "populuxe," the postwar American Dream—helped to load down the car with an average of forty-four pounds of surplus chrome for the mid-line Detroit product of the late 50s. Whereas [GM designer] Harley Earl's finny 1948 Cadillac was considered a bit much for the average Joe, by 1955 all of its most gratuitous features were also available on the humble Chevy. The 1957 Cadillac Eldorado Brougham, at $13,074 uninflated bucks, was a mobile [sultan's palace] hitched to a dashboard with a built-in tissue box, a vanity case, a lipstick that harmonized with the paint job, and a set of four gold-finished drinking cups. Along with the usual power accessories, deep-pile upholstery, padded interiors, coil springs, and barge-like proportions, the car offered the trappings of kingly ease to a culture that also gave the world the mink-handled beer can opener, the gold-plated charge-a-plate, whiskey-flavored toothpaste (for the morning after), radar-equipped fishing rods, and hair color kits with names like Golden Apricot Delight and Champagne Beige. The cars themselves were the largest hunks of luxury around, but there were other automotive manifestations of the yen for the posh: the pseudo-aristocratic [name] attached to models like the "Eldorado," dripping with fevered fantasies of gold; the delicious array of car colors that suggested a lush infinity of choices.

CHAPTER 5

TV, Beatniks, and Rock Rebellion

AMERICA'S DECADES

A Day in the Life of a 1954 TV Viewer

Richard D. Heldenfels

Television viewers of the 1990s would hardly recognize the TV of the early 1950s. Most programs were produced locally and commercials were relatively infrequent. Because a good television cost almost as much as a new car, families could afford only one television, usually in the form of a big, boxy piece of furniture. Once installed, the entire family would gather to watch whatever was broadcast on the two available channels.

Author Richard D. Heldenfels, a journalist and TV historian who writes for the *Akron Beacon Journal,* takes the reader back to 1954, when the television experience was brand new.

You are now part of a family that has set aside the newspaper stories of U.S. troop withdrawals from the Korean conflict, Suez Canal negotiations between Egypt and Great Britain, and that day's Rose Bowl confrontation between Michigan State and UCLA. The Christmas records, including a new one by Dean Martin, have been put away, tucked next to the mambo albums in the hi-fi cabinet. Mom has turned off the radio. Dad has stubbed out his Camel. . . . The occasion: The family is about to make its first journey into home television.

Naturally, everyone will travel together. Only about 3 percent of American homes have more than one TV. And the picture is in black-and-white. Although color programming has begun on a limited basis, no local station will be able to transmit it until summer; even then, the only color shows will come from the networks, with locally produced color shows still many months away.

Besides, the local dealers still do not have any color TVs and any one that you find will be expensive. The lowest estimates are $800, the highest $1,000 and more. Considering that a factory worker's gross salary is about $70 a week, a color TV is just a dream. . . .

In addition to living with a black-and-white image, viewing is going to be potluck, consisting of whatever happens to be on at the time you are watching. A home videotape recording system will not be available until 1965. TV production itself is either filmed, live, or on kinescope, a crude recording process of limited usefulness; although a videotape system was demonstrated in 1953, a workable one is still two years away. So forget those videotaped "instant replays" when you watch sports. . . .

Slow-Paced Programs with Few Commercials

Just by sitting in front of that television set, a family entered a relationship that was significantly different from the one between viewer and viewing in the nineties. While modern viewers occasionally sit as a family in front of the set, the proliferation of multiset homes, especially with small TVs, moves the viewing experience to the kitchen and bedroom, at once fragmenting the viewing and forcing the TV program to compete directly with other activities. The bond between TV and its audience is accordingly weaker now, the challenge much greater for the programmer. . . .

Modern TV has to be louder, flashier, and fancier to lure a viewer busy chopping carrots to a five-inch image under the kitchen cabinet. In the fifties, such was not the case. Even when the most frantic comedian was on the air, television moved at a more leisurely pace. With many programs live and the technology still limited, shows did not engage in the sort of jumpy cutting of the MTV age. The half-hour and hour-long programs of the day had more time to tell a story than their modern counterparts because commercials took only about six minutes out of a program hour, about half what they consume today. And since a single commercial usually ran a minute, there were fewer spots in a break; the National Association of Broadcasters' Television Code also recommended against running more than two spots per break. Although complaints about ad bombardment were loud in the early fifties, it was nothing compared to the shelling today.

The very act of watching TV in the fifties involved a commitment. An old newspaper cartoon showed various people, all stopped midway in their dressing or undressing, drawn into the living room by the hijinks on their TV; that sort of gathering does not happen when the TV is two steps from the closet. Similarly, the commitment to a single program was far stronger without a remote to allow a change of channel from across the room; it's wonderful what we viewers will tolerate when the alternative requires rising from a well-dug groove in the couch.

Two Channels for the Price of a Car

So the search for the perfect television took time and thought. You have considered RCA and Du Mont, General Electric and Olympia, Philco and Capehart, CBS-Columbia and Silvertone. Sears had a 17-inch Silvertone with mahogany veneer for $198.88, a 21-incher for $60 more. But Philco pushed a 21-incher for its "lowest price ever," $200.

To the modern consumer that should probably be "only" $200, but these are old-time dollars. A five-figure income is a dream for most Americans. Moreover, in the erratic economy of the early fifties, unemployment doubled between October 1953 and October 1954.

A three-bedroom home is selling for under $12,000, a

1948 Chevrolet is going for $495, ground beef is 39 cents a pound. The Bendix washing machine the family almost bought was "only" $169.95. What tipped the scales: the washing machine did not [feature entertainers such as] Arthur Godfrey.

Once the family decided the washer could wait a while, its dream TV became a fully equipped G.E. console set, with mahogany finish and half-doors to close over the TV screen; able to get VHF (Channels 2–13) and UHF (Channel 14 and beyond); and a big 21-inch picture, all for $439.95. And, as a bonus, you've started getting this magazine, TV Guide, not even a year old yet but promising insight into the wonderful world of TV.

So the moment has arrived. The family is gathered round. It's 7 A.M. and the test pattern gives way at last to something to watch.

Well, one thing to watch.

In January 1954 viewers in Schenectady can choose from a total of two TV stations, and then only if their set is equipped for both UHF and VHF reception. Nor is this all that unusual since the Federal Communications Commission froze the issue of station licenses from 1948 to 1952. Even after the FCC lifted the freeze, it did so by granting a lot of UHF licenses in communities where VHF had been the rule before.

The total number of stations, only 108 serving 63 television markets at the end of the freeze, will have tripled by the end of 1954, but the old-line stations will have had the advantage of time, experience, and long-standing ties with the four commercial networks. In your city, the VHF station—G.E.-owned WRGB—has affiliation agreements with ABC, CBS, NBC, and Du Mont, picking what it wants from the available programs; the lone UHF competitor (which will be joined by two others before the year's end) has to settle for shows that the VHF station does not want. For that reason—and because of its tight financial situation this uphill competitive battle has caused—the UHF station, WROW, does not even sign on until 1:30 P.M. on New

Year's Day, and that early only because it has a football bowl game to carry; come Monday it will be back to its usual sign-on time of 5 P.M.

Not that things are all that great at the big stations. *Time* magazine has recently suggested "TV broadcasting may be nearing the saturation point" because an FCC survey of eighty-three older stations concluded that only sixteen are making money. And that's before stations around the nation had to face the additional outlays to make color telecasts possible.

But at least WRGB has a day full of programs, starting with NBC's *Today* show in the morning, then going into CBS's soap operas, plus shows from the other networks as well as local productions. Nor are local shows confined to news; television is a local thing across the board.

Hours of Local Programming

The existing networks did not fill the kinds of hours they do now. Prime time—which started at 7 P.M. on ABC and Du Mont, 7:30 on CBS and NBC—was a rich field overall but still had gaps; Du Mont's schedule was a checkerboard of programs and empty spaces for stations to fill. The existing network newscasts, only fifteen minutes long, were also in prime time rather than the early evening hours. *Today* was the lone network early-morning show, although CBS would make its first try at a morning program in March 1954 (then give it up three years later after numerous, unsuccessful changes).

NBC had ventured into late-night several years ago with *Broadway Open House* but its late-night standard, *Tonight,* did not begin its network run until September 1954. When *Television* magazine tried to assess *Tonight*'s chances for success, it studied how local late-night shows were doing in some markets, among them Soupy Sales's *Soupy's On* in Detroit, *Pantomime Parade* in Cincinnati, *Polka Revue* in Cleveland, and "hillbilly singer" Ernie Lee's show in Dayton.

When *TV Guide* announced its awards for the 1953–54 season, three pages were devoted to the network winners and four to outstanding local personalities in the twenty-four cities where *TV Guide* circulated. The local winners included a children's show host in Milwaukee, a comedienne from Dallas, a singer from Fort Lauderdale, an educational filmmaker in New York and a couple hosting a show for teenagers in Denver. Bandleader Lawrence Welk

 TV Obscenity in 1951

From its inception in the 1950s, civic and religious leaders complained about the content of programs. Shows considered innocent now were labeled lewd and obscene in their time. J. Fred MacDonald, curator of the Chicago Museum of Broadcast Communications and professor of history at Northeastern Illinois University, explores what the Citizens' Television Code of 1952 deemed objectionable material.

It was sexual expression that . . . aroused moralists threatened by the intrusive new medium [of television]. Typically, a Roman Catholic bishop in Michigan praised TV in 1951 as "one of the great achievements of our age," then blasted it as a "sex-promoter" that popularized "sex artists whose stock in trade is to make sex [antics] before innocent children in their homes." According to the Church official, despite its technological brilliance television was "doing the work of the devil by bootlegging into homes foulness and obscenity."

One of the bolder public moves against video imagery and language occurred in Chicago in mid-1950 when the weekly magazine *TV Forecast* spearheaded the creation of the National Television Review Board. The purpose of this panel of prominent citizens was to rate programs in terms of their effect on family life. Soon the Board publicly condemned shows it felt objectionable, among them [children's show] *Howdy Doody* ("loud . . . confused . . . senseless . . . clown's role too feminine"), *Juvenile Jury* ("bad taste . . . smart-aleck kids should be spanked instead

was a winner for his musical show in Los Angeles, Soupy Sales for his Detroit shows.

In addition, network shows were identified less with their broadcasters than with their sponsors, who could put their names in the shows' titles *(Camel News Caravan, Kraft Television Theatre)*, display their products on the

---

of applauded"), wrestling ("phony contest . . . unsportsmanlike tactics . . . glorifies sadism"), and *Leave It to the Girls* ("gowns cut too low . . . ridicules marriage . . . excessive frivolity concerning family authority and customs"). By early 1952 the Board issued its "Citizens' Television Code," complete with a twelve-point guide to "what shall be deemed objectionable":

- Immoral, lewd, and suggestive words and actions, as well as indecency in dress.
- A deliberate presentation of vulgar and sordid situations.
- Irreverence toward religion or patriotic symbols where it is not essential to a dramatic situation.
- Excessive bad taste in words and actions, deliberately projected for their own effect.
- Excessive frivolity concerning established traditions of family authority and customs.
- Malicious derision of racial or national groups.
- Undue glorification of criminals and undesirables.
- Excessive bloodshed, violence, and cruelty.
- Excessive noise, confusion, and tumult to a point where it disrupts normal family relationships.
- Any ideas, situations, or presentations that essentially injure the dignity of God and mankind and the inalienable right of human integrity.
- Shows that tend to glamorize false values.
- Disloyal or subversive sentiments that might injure the United States.

J. Fred MacDonald, *One Nation Under Television*. New York: Pantheon, 1990.

sets, and weave their commercials into the program itself. A Rhino videotape celebrating the worst in television history includes the fifties quiz show *Penny to a Million* whose cigarette-company sponsor was mentioned several times in a series of questions about tobacco.

And finally, given the relative rarity of stations, and the even rarer examples of successful ones, local stations had more power in choosing and scheduling programs, including those of their own making that might more readily appeal to local viewers. Over time, as networks locked stations into lucrative but exclusive agreements, as the networks began to fill time slots they had previously ignored, and as it proved cheaper for stations to buy shows than to produce them, the situation would change. One TV veteran later said:

> You could do the best local entertainment program you could, with good performers and beautiful sets. And half an hour later, Dean Martin could go on and stand in front of a curtain and get five times the audience.

Sitcoms, Dramas, News, and Soaps

But for the moment, local programming was a major distinction between 1954 TV and what viewers are getting 40 years later. To talk about other differences let's look at some genres:

Sitcoms: This would be most familiar to modern viewers, since shows like *Ozzie & Harriet, Make Room for Daddy* (later called *The Danny Thomas Show*), *Jack Benny,* and *Burns & Allen* survive in various formats and venues to this day; the most popular show of the period was *I Love Lucy,* in 1994 enjoying renewed attention through reruns on Nick at Nite. Groucho Marx's long-running show You *Bet Your Life* (in its heart a situation comedy with Groucho playing a rascally but lovable quiz-show host) was also on view. Other shows, much admired in their day, are less well remembered; *Mr. Peepers,* a comedy starring Wally Cox as a teacher, still has ardent fans but is little seen because, done live, it survives only in un-telegenic kinescopes.

Drama: There were dramatic series, most notably the landmark police show *Dragnet* and its imitators. . . . But the dramatic strength of the period lay in the live anthologies such as *Studio One, Philco-Goodyear Playhouse,* and *U.S. Steel Hour,* as well as lesser lights such as the live-and-film anthology *Schlitz Playhouse.* The anthologies filled a very similar role to the modern television movie (which did not yet exist in 1954)—bringing diversity to the schedule and showcasing well-known actors—but the sensibility was not from the movies but the New York stage.

Whether dealing with grand historical moments or small personal stories, anthologies also provided an opening in television for actors, directors, and most significantly writers such as Rod Serling, Horton Foote, Reginald Rose, and Paddy Chayefsky, who became marquee names on the small screen. And because new plays were needed each week, other writers had opportunities to get work and gain fame that would be far harder to come by in the more rigid world of dramatic series to come.

News: Two major weeknight newscasts on CBS and NBC were already on the air; although just fifteen minutes long, their basic format was that of the modern newscast. *See It Now,* a weekly half-hour hosted by Edward R. Murrow, examined stories with the range and detail that would later be seen in network news magazines. Plus there were commentary shows with various newspaper columnists, the early-morning *Today* show, and Sunday public affairs series such as *Meet the Press.*

Daytime: The soap opera was making the transition from radio to television, but the talk show was not the force it is today. Instead of talk, one had variety shows, such as those hosted by Arthur Godfrey and Bob Crosby, which mingled music, games, and a bit of chatter, all aimed at the supposedly homebound [housewife]. Later in 1954 NBC launched *Home,* an all-purpose information show for women, as well.

Daytime TV was also considered a province for children at home. As anyone who ever unrolled a red strip of black-dotted pistol caps knows, the little ones feasted on Westerns with stars such as Roy Rogers and Gene Autry. They also enjoyed puppet shows (cartoons had not yet taken over children's TV), ventriloquist Paul Winchell, the early space opera *Captain Video, The Adventures of Superman* and such thoughtful fare as *Ding Dong School,* which on recent examination seemed a prototype for *Mr. Rogers' Neighborhood.* . . .

Sports, Religious Programming, and Variety

Sports: Athletic feats, notably prime-time boxing and wrestling, had been crucial to the early success of television; by 1954 boxing had a lot of clout but wrestling was coming to the end of its first run of success. Tennis, hockey, basketball, football, and the most important game of all, baseball, had places on the schedule. But they had not swallowed up the weekend television schedule to the extent they would in later years. Major sports leaders feared that television, even as it brought in an audience that might not be able to see a live game, would prove fatal to those places with flourishing local venues. And as critic Ron Powers has written, some elitist network executives saw sports as something that dirtied their hands.

Cultural programs: One advantage to the sports vacuum on Sundays was that it opened up program hours to public affairs and cultural shows. Sunday was the home to televised operas and symphony concerts as well as the classic series *Omnibus,* a mingling of all sorts of intellectual fare and hosted by the urbane Alistair Cooke, later linked to PBS as host of *Masterpiece Theatre.* But opera also had a small place in prime time, and both jazz and Broadway music—more commonly heard in these days before rock 'n' roll entered the mainstream—were often featured around the dial. (In a wonderful bit on *Caesar's Hour,* jazz was ultimately defined as "a beautiful woman whose older brother is a policeman.")

178

Religion: Sunday shows with religious themes appeared on the networks and local stations; prime time also had its religious stars, especially Catholic Bishop Fulton J. Sheen.

Variety: A term that encompasses shows with a heavy comedic bent, others with a musical twist, shows with immensely talented hosts and another whose host could barely speak (Ed Sullivan), the variety show offered some of the most spectacular moments in TV in the forties and fifties; for that matter the "spectaculars" (later known as specials) that began to appear in 1954 were often variety shows held together by the barest of plots.

In any case the shows mingled comedy, music, and other forms of entertainment in various formulas: *Colgate Comedy Hour* boasted hosts such as Eddie Cantor, Martin and Lewis, and Abbott and Costello but still found room for song; one Cantor-hosted show featured the cast (that night including Eddie Fisher and Frank Sinatra) singing Harold Arlen tunes with the composer himself at the piano. Ed Sullivan—well, you never knew what to expect from the newspaper columnist turned impresario (and neither, judging from the recollections of people who worked on the show, did the staff of what was then called *Toast of the Town).* Jackie Gleason was demonstrating his mastery of sketch comedy on his series, including in a series of "Honeymooners" sketches that would lead to a separate show in 1955; Sid Caesar was doing the impossible with a grand ensemble of writers and actors on *Your Show of Shows* and *Caesar's Hour;* Milton Berle was still at it; master clown Red Skelton had a weekly half-hour.

For all that TV had to offer in 1954, the modern viewer would still feel some disorientation, when the newscasts ended after their brief turns, when variety shows (now so rarely seen) popped up with such regularity, when the black and white images were unrelieved by more than a smattering of color.

The Birth of Rock and Roll

Adam Woog

In the following excerpt from his book *The History of Rock and Roll*, Adam Woog describes how during the 1950s—a time of strict conformity—the wild rhythms of rock and roll music painted a rainbow of color across an otherwise black-and-white decade. The music that came to be known as rock and roll first emanated from the rhythm and blues (R&B) played in backroom bars in African American neighborhoods. When performers combined R&B with the so-called hillbilly twang of the rural south, rock and roll was born.

During an era of strict segregation, black rock and roll music became immensely popular with white suburban teenagers. By 1955, black artists such as Chuck Berry, Fats Domino, and Little Richard were enjoying unprecedented success. White artists soon followed—Elvis Presley's string of hits made him a household name, and rock and roll became the defining element of a new teen culture.

The exact point at which rock and roll coalesced is shrouded in mystery, and there are many worthy contenders for the title of first rock-and-roll record.

Some music scholars say that it was Roy Brown's 1948 R&B hit "Good Rockin' Tonight." (The same song was

Reprinted from *The History of Rock and Roll*, by Adam Woog (San Diego: Lucent Books, 1999) with permission.

later an even bigger hit for Elvis Presley.) Others point to "Rock All Night Long" by a New York vocal group, the Ravens, released the same year. Still others champion a 1949 single, "Rock Awhile," by an obscure Houston guitarist, Goree Carter.

Each of these records had the necessary basic ingredients, and all are impressive candidates. Perhaps the strongest contender, however, is "Rocket '88," recorded in Memphis in March 1951. With its grainy vocal, fuzzy guitar sound, wild sax solo, and subject matter (the singer's car), it is a superb prediction of the direction of early rock and roll.

The leader of the band behind "Rocket '88" was Ike Turner. Years before he formed his famous soul revue with then-wife Tina, Ike was a popular bandleader in the Memphis area. On "Rocket '88," however, saxophonist Jackie Brenston was the singer, and the record is credited to him.

The story behind the song's distinctive guitar sound illustrates the casual nature of pop record production in the 1950s. Lead guitarist Willie Kizart's amp had fallen from his car on the way to the studio, and the speaker cone burst. Producer Sam Phillips, later a legendary figure through his work with Elvis Presley, recalls, "It would probably have taken a couple of days [to fix it], so we started playing around with the damn thing. I stuffed a little paper in there where the speaker cone was ruptured, and it sounded good."

The Independents

"Rocket '88" and other "protorock" records, for all their charms, were strictly localized phenomena. Ike Turner was a star around Memphis, but neither he nor any other early rock artist was yet able to score a national hit.

One reason for this was that their recordings were made by small companies with shoestring budgets and limited distribution. None of the big record companies thought that R&B was worth pushing since the vast majority of the pop audience was white—at least that part of the pop audience with money to spend. The big record companies concentrated instead on mainstream pop.

This left R&B open to the small, independent labels. In Los Angeles the Aladdin and Specialty labels recorded R&B singers like Amos Milburn and Larry Williams. In Memphis, Sam Phillips nurtured his Sun imprint. Labels like Ace were documenting the lively New Orleans sound.

The Chess brothers, based in Chicago, were typical. They visited the Deep South twice a year to record musicians for their small, blues-based Chess label. They carried with them a cumbersome tape recorder powered by a portable gas generator, so that they could record anywhere. More than once they lugged their equipment into the middle of a cotton field to record a musician on his lunch break.

These little labels, however, lacked the resources to take their music across the country. Rock and roll existed, and it was ready for America to discover it, but a national hit was needed first.

"Rock Around the Clock"

That honor went to 1953's "Crazy Man Crazy," the first certified rock and roll record to make the *Billboard* pop charts.

The singer was a former country musician named Bill Haley. The fact that he was a white man playing in a black style doubtless helped Haley's breakthrough success. Dave Bartholomew, a New Orleans producer, says, "We had rhythm and blues for many, many a year, and here come in a couple of white people and they call it rock and roll, and it was rhythm and blues all the time!"

Haley followed his hit with others, including a tame version of "Shake, Rattle, and Roll," a song first popularized by blues shouter Big Joe Turner. Haley's "Rock Around the Clock" became a number-one hit after it was featured in *The Blackboard Jungle*, a popular movie about teenage rebellion.

Haley's career was short, however. Uncharismatic, pudgy, slightly balding, and self-conscious about a blind eye, he never had the chance to capitalize on his stardom. His wooden singing and competent but dull band, meanwhile, paled in comparison with the unbridled energy of later musicians.

Many fans and scholars have down-played Haley's role in rock history. Nonetheless, his tentative blend of white and black styles made him an important rock-and-roll pioneer. In an interview in the 1970s, Haley wistfully commented on his lack of recognition: "The story has got pretty crowded as to who was the Father of Rock and Roll. I haven't done much in life except that. And I'd like to get credit for it."

The First True Rock and Roller?

Even as Haley was beginning to fade from the public eye, big things were stirring elsewhere. Between 1953 and 1955, the first true rockers—a tidal wave that included Chuck Berry, Fats Domino, and Little Richard—swept across America.

The honor paid to Chuck Berry as the first inductee to the Rock and Roll Hall of Fame is an indication of his importance to the music. Many consider Berry the first true rock and roller because of both his music and his bad-boy personal life; he has been the center of controversy for decades, including two stints in prison.

Berry's formative years demonstrated the powerful effect of intermingled regional styles. Growing up in St. Louis, Missouri, he absorbed everything from Chicago blues and Midwest jump bands to southern country.

He later worked as a beautician while leading a blues band and writing songs he hoped would appeal to teenagers. His break came when Chess Records bought his "Ida Red"; the Chess executives didn't like the title, however, and convinced Berry to change it to "Maybellene." The song, released in 1955, reached the top ten and was the first of Berry's many hits.

The best of Berry's songs are models of economy and wit, full of clever wordplay and simple but potent images. "Maybellene," "School Day," "Sweet Little Sixteen," "Johnny B. Goode," "The Promised Land," and "Roll

Over Beethoven"—to name only a handful—went on to become a part of America's pop heritage. Rock critic and journalist Ben Fong-Torres writes that they are "a body of highly American imagery from which rock & roll continues to feed."

Berry's patented guitar licks and manic "duckwalk" set a performance standard for years to come. Like T-Bone Walker before him, Berry was an innovator whose influence is still felt. Rock critic and journalist Robert Christgau wryly notes, "He taught George Harrison [of the Beatles] and Keith Richards [of the Rolling Stones] to play guitar long before he met either."

"The Fat Man"

New Orleans has been the cradle of many memorable musical styles, including a vibrant R&B scene. In the early 1950s, that scene produced a musician who perfectly summed up the city's rich mixture of black, white, French, Spanish, and Creole cultures—and who also rocked.

Antoine "Fats" Domino began building a strong local reputation with his first single, "The Fat Man," in 1949, when he was twenty-one. By the time rock and roll began to be felt nationwide, therefore, he was a seasoned musician, and his records were routinely selling over a half-million copies apiece.

Domino did not have a national hit, however, until "Ain't That a Shame" in 1955. The tunes that followed—"Blue Monday," "Blueberry Hill," "I'm Walkin'"—proved he could sustain his hitmaking on a national level. Including his last million-seller, "Walkin' to New Orleans" in 1960, Domino racked up twenty-three gold singles (singles that sold a million or more). In all, he sold over 65 million records, more than any 1950s rock pioneer except Elvis Presley.

Domino's charm came from several sources. His genial, sweetly rotund persona was never threatening, unlike other rockers. Musically, his records were an appealing blend of his unique half-blues and half-country piano style, loose but rocking arrangements, and distinctive, lazy Creole accent. The combination made perfect pop records, both as individual as a thumbprint and as familiar as an old shoe. New Orleans studio owner and engineer Cosimo Matassa comments, "Domino, he was creative. No matter what he does comes through. He could be singing the national anthem, you'd still know by the time he said two words it was him, obviously, unmistakably, and pleasurably him."

The Georgia Peach

Little Richard (nicknamed "the Georgia Peach" for his Georgia roots) may not have been the most gifted of the early rockers, but he was the wildest. Richard ironically called himself "the Bronze Liberace." The title reflected how his gleefully over-the-top style (towering hair, heavy makeup, flamboyant wardrobe, and teasing sexuality) echoed that of Liberace, a pop pianist who had delighted and scandalized a previous generation. No one had more attitude than Little Richard.

Richard Penniman was born in Macon, Georgia, into a religious family. They listened to mainstream pop, but Richard had to sneak around to play "the devil's music"—the raunchy material that he secretly loved. He recalls, "Bing Crosby, 'Pennies from Heaven,' Ella Fitzgerald, was all I heard. And I knew there was something that could be louder than that, but I didn't know where to find it. And I found it was me."

Richard toured with medicine shows and R&B bands before developing his own flashy style and forming a band. His first big hit, "Tutti Frutti," sold a respectable half-million singles in 1955.

"Tutti Frutti" and successors like "Long Tall Sally" and "Good Golly Miss Molly," with their nonsense lyrics and rough energy, made the Georgia Peach a star, especially among fans who delighted in scandalizing their parents. Little Richard also became famous for his excessive on-tour partying; as he recalls, "The river was running. The river of loot. And I was on the bank."

But Little Richard was always torn between two extremes: the extravagant rock-and-roll lifestyle and a deeply devout religious faith. In the years since he exploded on the scene, the Georgia Peach has periodically abandoned music in favor of Bible study, popping up now and again to loudly proclaim, to anyone who will listen, that he is the true father of rock and roll.

A King Is Born

Chuck Berry, Fats Domino, and Little Richard were only the tip of the iceberg. Between 1955 and 1958, they were joined by dozens of other rockers. The roll call is long and distinguished, but one man, more than any other, defined this golden age of classic rock and roll.

Perhaps no other performer has had a greater impact on pop culture than Elvis Presley. More than twenty years after his death, his name, his face, and his music still evoke instant recognition even in distant corners of the world. For many people Elvis was—and is—rock and roll. In a saying frequently attributed to Bruce Springsteen, "There have been contenders, but there is only one King."

Elvis Presley

Elvis did not invent rock and roll. He was not the first to bring black and white musical styles together. It can be argued that he was not the music's most gifted singer. Nor did he write his own songs, relying instead on other (often mediocre) writers. Nonetheless, Elvis remains the single most important person in the development of rock and roll.

This is because he was gifted not only as a performer and a synthesizer of styles but also as a popularizer. He was the first person to bring rock and roll to a truly widespread, mixed-race audience by successfully merging the intensity of black music with a mournful hillbilly sound. In so doing, he introduced rock and roll to the world.

As a teenager fresh out of high school and working as a truck driver in Memphis, Presley made his first recording at a local studio. According to legend, it was a gift for his mother.

His voice caught the attention of the studio's owner. Sam Phillips, the producer of Ike Turner's "Rocket '88" and a fanatical champion of black music, had often remarked that he could make a fortune if he found a singer with the passion of a black artist and a face that would appeal to white audiences. He thought that Elvis might just be that singer.

Phillips teamed the young singer with two professional musicians, guitarist Scotty Moore and bassist Bill Black. After months of practice they released their first single in 1954. Its two songs reflected Presley's ability to span white and black styles. One side was a blues song, "That's All Right (Mama)," and the other was a sped-up version of a country waltz, "Blue Moon of Kentucky."

The record was a regional hit, and Presley's fame slowly grew. Under the direction of a wily manager, Colonel Tom Parker, the singer's career took off. After his Sun contract was sold to a major record company, RCA, for the unheard-of sum of thirty-five thousand dollars, Presley's "Heartbreak Hotel" was his first national hit in 1956—and the first volley in Parker's scheme to make "his boy" into the most successful entertainment figure of all time.

Rockabilly Lives

When Elvis left Sam Phillips's care, the producer's other protégés carried on the style he and Elvis had more or less invented: rockabilly.

In the late 1950s many southern musicians experimented with their own blends of country and rock. Standouts included the exquisite harmonies of the Everly Brothers, the heartbreakingly pure voice of Roy Orbison, and the playful, hiccuping vocals of Buddy Holly. Rockabilly, however, was the most radical of these fusions.

It had an unmistakable sound: up-tempo, with accented offbeats from a slapping bass, vocals with plenty of echo (the singers often sounded like they were in a sewer pipe), and snappy lyrics: "My gal is red hot! Your gal ain't doodly squat!" Looks were also important; musicians and fans alike dressed in elaborate "cat clothes" and slicked their hair into greasy pompadours.

There were many hopefuls, including Charlie Feathers, Gene Vincent, and Billy Lee Riley, but Carl Perkins, a gifted singer-writer-guitarist, was the heir apparent to rockabilly stardom. Though Elvis later made the song famous, Perkins's version of "Blue Suede Shoes" (which he wrote) was the first record to top the R&B, country, and pop charts simultaneously. Unfortunately, Perkins suffered a serious car accident just as the record was peaking, and his career never reached the heights once promised.

The wild rockabilly persona, meanwhile, was best illustrated by one performer. Jerry Lee Lewis, out of Ferriday, Louisiana, wasn't called "the Killer" for nothing.

In an era already dominated by the guitar, Lewis played an unlikely instrument: the piano. But he played it in an unforgettable way—with his feet and his fists, kicking over the stool, jumping on the piano, all the while growling and crooning into the microphone.

Lewis's handful of singles for Sun, including "Whole Lotta Shakin' Goin' On" and "Great Balls of Fire," remain definitive recordings of the era.

Offstage he was equally famous for his nonstop drinking, womanizing, gun-toting, and overall rowdy behavior. Many critics feel he was as talented as his great rival Elvis, and that he might have become as big a commercial success were it not for his relentlessly threatening personal style.

Moondog Spreads the Word

In the early 1950s television was still a novelty. Radio was the main outlet for rockabilly and other kinds of new music exploding out of Los Angeles, Nashville, Memphis, Chicago, and New Orleans.

At the time few national radio networks existed. Instead, individual stations maintained loyal regional followings. Disc jockeys decided what songs to play and how often to play them. But stations and their audiences were also fairly strictly divided along racial lines at that point, and no white-oriented station touched rock and roll until Alan Freed came along.

Freed was hosting a classical show on WJW in Cleveland, Ohio, when he noticed in a record store that white teens were snapping up the latest rock-and-roll records. Freed talked his station manager into letting him host a show that spotlighted the music, and *Moondog's Rock 'n' Roll Party* debuted in June 1951.

But the Kids Like It

David P. Szatmary's Rockin' in Time *contains this summary of the typical critical reaction to Elvis Presley.*

"In one review Jack Gould, the television critic for the New York *Times*, wrote 'Mr. Presley has no discernable singing ability. His specialty is rhythm, songs which he renders in an undistinguished whine; his phrasing, if it can be called that, consists of the stereo-typed variations that go with a beginner's aria in a bathtub. . . . His one specialty is an accented movement of the body that heretofore has been primarily identified with the repertoire of the blonde bombshells of the burlesque runway. The gyration never had anything to do with the world of popular music and still doesn't.' Jack O'Brien of the New York *Journal-American* agreed that 'Elvis Presley wiggled and wiggled with such abdominal gyrations that burlesque bombshell Georgia Southern really deserves equal time to reply in gyrating kind. He can't sing a lick, makes up for vocal shortcomings with the weirdest and plainly planned, suggestive animation short of an aborigine's mating dance.'"

David P. Szatmary, *Rockin' in Time: A Social History of Rock and Roll.* Englewood Cliffs, NJ: Prentice-Hall, 1987.

The term *rock and roll* had been used in the black community for years, as both slang for sex and as a musical term. In 1946 *Billboard* had described R&B bandleader Joe Liggins's single "Sugar Lump" as "right rhythmic rock and roll music." On Freed's show, however, the phrase was introduced to a mainstream audience for probably the first time.

Freed cultivated a crazed manner to go with the music: howling at the moon, beating his fist in time to the music in front of an open mike, talking in nonstop jive patter, and drinking openly while on the air. His show was an immediate hit with its target audience of "moondog daddies and crazy kittens," and Freed was soon imitated by others, including Dewey Phillips in Memphis, Poppa Stoppa in New Orleans, and the gravel-voiced Bob "Wolfman Jack" Smith, whose high-powered "pirate" station in Mexico could be heard as far away as Canada.

Playing black music for white audiences, in those times of strong racial segregation, was a bold move. Freed did it because he wanted a hit show, but he also genuinely liked the music. "Cousin" Brucie Morrow, another DJ of the era, remarks, "Alan Freed became one of the bravest men ever to be a part of the record industry. . . . It was a kind of integrity that led him to play the R&B music that no one else would touch."

"Whaddya Got?"

Radio could get the message out, but rock and roll would not have flourished without the explosive development of teen culture in America after the war, and its acceptance of the music.

Thanks to a strong postwar economy, American teens had far fewer responsibilities and far more leisure time and money than ever before. Translated into purchasing power, for the first time in history teens formed a pool of consumers controlling billions of disposable dollars.

Naturally, before long products specifically for teens appeared in quantity. As rock historian Paul Friedlander writes, "American business, recognizing the existence of a new consumer group, rushed to fill the void, providing 'essential' items such as clothes, cosmetics, fast food, cars—and music."

Records (mostly singles with some long-play albums), radios (bulky table models or the thrilling new transistors), and hi-fi sets (stereo was still in the future) all absorbed the entertainment dollars teens were spending. However, the music industry often found it difficult to produce music that satisfied teens.

The pop music turned out by the major record labels was, almost without exception, bland and predictable. Teenagers preferred what they heard on small, scruffy, independent labels—the far more exciting and dangerous sounds of R&B and rock and roll.

The new music struck a chord of rebellion against the conformist, complacent society of the postwar years, an attitude summed up by Marlon Brando's famous line in *The Wild One*. In that movie a waitress asks Brando, who plays the leader of a motorcycle gang, what he's rebelling against. Brando coolly replies, "Whaddya got?"

An Evil Influence

Naturally, adults were disconcerted by such attitudes. How could kids be so rebellious when they had everything they wanted? Thus was laid one of the fundamental cornerstones of rock and roll: its long tradition of driving the old folks up the wall.

Parents and authorities, especially conservative lawmakers and clergy, increasingly railed against the influence of rock and roll on impressionable youth. Juvenile delinquents, race mixing, violence, vandalism—it was all clearly tied in with the music. Typical was a 1956 comment by the Reverend Albert Carter, a Pentecostal minister:

> The effect of rock and roll in young people is to turn them into devil worshippers; to stimulate self-expression through sex; to provoke lawlessness, impair nervous stability and

destroy the sanctity of marriage. It is an evil influence on the youth of our country.

The established music-industry response was to make rock tamer, more acceptable to a mainstream audience. It was the first attempt—but by no means the last—to tamp down rock and roll's unruly energy.

Beat Poets Give Birth to the Hippie Movement

Andrew Jamison and Ron Eyeman

According to authors Andrew Jamison and Ron Eyeman, popular culture of the 1950s was dominated by the musical revolution of rock and roll. The era also experienced a literary revolution in the so-called Beat movement emerging in New York City, San Francisco, and other large cities. The self-appointed leader of the Beat generation was poet Allen Ginsberg, who, along with William Burroughs, Jack Kerouac, Lawrence Ferlinghetti, and other writers provided inspiration to millions of college-bound teens.

The Beats were the first to protest the blandness and conformity of the era. While most Americans moved to the suburbs, the Beats lived in cities, embraced black jazz culture, and pioneered what would later become the "hippie" counterculture. Beats saw suburbia as a prison and saw themselves as poets in a land of materialism.

In the late fifties and early sixties, inspired by the paperback books of the Beat poets, tens of thousands of suburban youths cast aside their button-down past to become beatniks, obsessed with writing poetry, hitchhiking across country, and trying to find nirvana in the neon American night.

Andrew Jamison and Ron Eyeman are American scholars at Lund University in Sweden. Together they have written several books about social movements.

In the midst of the Second World War, three pilgrims from as different social backgrounds as one could probably find among white Americans met by chance in a Manhattan apartment. What drew William S. Burroughs, Jr., Irwin Allen Ginsberg, and Jean Louis (Jack) Kerouac together was a feeling of being outside the main drift of American society. All three were sitting out a popular war while their fellows rushed to participate; all three were alienated from the careers their families and American society had planned for them. In addition, they all shared a love of literature and a taste for life on the social margins.

The scion of a wealthy Protestant, St. Louis family and many years older than Ginsberg and Kerouac, Burroughs had already gathered a range of life and literary experience and a sophistication that enraptured the two younger men. He had taken a degree in English literature at Harvard and studied medicine in Vienna, before finding his way to the shadowy underworld of drug dealers and small-time thieves around Times Square in midtown Manhattan and in the bohemian community in Greenwich Village. These two sides of Burroughs—the educated snob and the low-life deviant—fascinated the middle-class Ginsberg more than the working-class Kerouac, who had come to Columbia on a football scholarship. Ginsberg came to Columbia and to New York City from nearby Paterson, New Jersey, where his father, a moderately well-known poet, worked as a high school English teacher. Ginsberg's mother moved in and out of mental hospitals. Both of his parents were first-generation immigrants, the children of Russian Jews who were also active in radical politics. Louis Ginsberg, Allen's father, had been a socialist . . . while his mother, Naomi, attended Communist party meetings and defended Stalin. . . . The young Ginsberg grew up amid constant political squabbles as well as the anxiety surrounding his mother's mental health. In typical street socialist fashion, he mixed the immigrant desire for respectability and social mobility with political conscience, entering Columbia as a prelaw student. It was his older brother, however, who became the lawyer; Allen Ginsberg gravitated to the English department.

Questioning Literary Traditions

Located near Harlem in upper Manhattan, Columbia University and the promise of higher education provided the justification for the move into New York City for Ginsberg and thousands like him, including Kerouac and, for that matter, a young musician named Miles Davis. New York offered, as well, a variety of subcultures that could nourish the development of an alternative vision. Besides the Greenwich Village environment, the traditional home of cultural radicalism, where Burroughs and Ginsberg first met and to whose gay community they both continually returned, the proximity of Columbia to [the African American neighborhood of] Harlem provided another essential linkage. Columbia students in search of adventure and a lively experience outside their normal, middle-class upbringing did not have to look very far. Both Kerouac and Ginsberg were soon under the spell of Harlem nightlife and especially its [jazz] music.

Columbia's English department was at that time one of the most respected in the country. Ginsberg's first criticisms of American culture were formulated against the background of what he learned there. . . . Both Ginsberg and Kerouac took . . . formalism . . . as their main enemy, as they developed the spontaneous style of writing that was to become the characteristic trademark of the Beats. In their articulation of what they came to call the "New Vision," they drew inspiration from romantic poets, especially Baudelaire and Rimbaud. . . .

The New Vision set out to challenge the traditional view of American literature being taught at Columbia, taking its cue from the culture found on the streets of New York as interpreted through the spontaneous energy of the young artist. . . . The attempt to seek refuge in art was, of course, not new. What was distinct about the New Vision was . . . that the emphasis was put on individual spontaneity and the rejection of all inhibition and repression.

On the Road with Kerouac

Beat novelist Jack Kerouac wrote On the Road *in such a frenzy that he did not have time to stop and change sheets of paper in his typewriter. Instead he fed one long roll of butcher paper into the machine from beginning to end. The result became a classic example of Beat life.*

What is that feeling when you're driving away from people and they recede on the plaint till you see their specks dispersing?—it's the too-huge world vaulting us, and it's good-by. But we lean forward to the next crazy venture beneath the skies.

We wheeled through the sultry old light of Algiers, [Louisiana] back on the ferry, back toward the mud-splashed, crabbed old ships across the river, back on Canal, and out; on a two-lane highway to Baton Rouge in purple darkness; swung west there, crossed the Mississippi at a place called Port Allen. Port Allen—where the river's all rain and roses in a misty pinpoint darkness and where we swung around a circular drive in yellow foglight and suddenly saw the great black body below a bridge and crossed eternity again. What is the Mississippi River? a washed clod in the rainy night, a soft plopping from drooping Missouri banks, a dissolving, a riding of the tide down the eternal waterbed, a contribution to brown foams, a voyaging past endless vales and trees and levees, down along, down along, by Memphis, Greenville, Eudora, Vicksburg, Natchez, Port Allen, and Port Orleans and Port of the Deltas, by Potash, Venice, and the Night's Great Gulf, and out.

With the radio on to a mystery program, and as I looked out the window and saw a sign that said USE COOPER'S PAINT and I said, "Okay, I will," we rolled across the hoodwink night of the Louisiana plains—Lawtell, Eunice, Kinder, and DeQuincy, western rickety towns becoming more bayou-like as we reached the Sabine. In Old Opelousas I went into a grocery store to buy bread and cheese while Dean saw to gas and oil. It was just a shack; I could hear the family eating supper in the back. I waited a minute;

they went on talking. I took bread and cheese and slipped out the door. We had barely enough money to make Frisco. Meanwhile Dean took a carton of cigarettes from the gas station and we were stocked for the voyage—gas, oil, cigarettes, and food. Crooks don't know. He pointed the car straight down the road. . . .

The country turned strange and dark near Deweyville. Suddenly we were in the swamps.

"Man, do you imagine what it would be like if we found a jazzpoint in these swamps, with great big black fellas moanin' guitar blues and drinking snakejuice and makin signs at us?"

"Yes!"

There were mysteries around here. The car was going over a dirt road elevated off the swamps that dropped on both sides and drooped with vines. We pawed an apparition; it was a Negro man in a white shirt walking along with his arms upspread to the inky firmament. He must have been praying or calling down a curse. We zoomed right by; I looked out the back window to see his white eyes. "Whoo!" said Dean. "Look out. We better not stop in this here country." At one point we got stuck at a crossroads and stopped the car anyway. Dean turned off the headlamps. We were surrounded by a great forest of viny trees in which we could almost hear the slither of a million copperheads. The only thing we could see was the red ampere button on the Hudson dashboard. Marylou squealed with fright. We began laughing maniac laughs to scare her. We were scared too. We wanted to get out of this mansion of the snake, this mireful drooping dark, and zoom on back to familiar American ground and cowtowns. There was a smell of oil and dead water in the air. This was a manuscript of the night we couldn't read. An owl hooted. We took a chance on one of the dirt roads, and pretty soon we were crossing the evil old Sabine River that is responsible for all these swamps. With amazement we saw great structures of light ahead of us. "Texas! It's Texas! Beaumont oil town!" Huge oil tanks and refineries loomed like cities in the oily fragrant air.

Jack Kerouac, *On the Road.* New York: New American Library, 1957.

Energy and Alienation

Like their European predecessors, art was seen to express an entire form of life and thus should offer a guide to living. Their art was confessional as well as expressive: what they sought was not a pure art of sensuality but more nearly the very opposite, a raw art of an almost primitive nature, to be found among the outsiders and the outcasts of the mass society. Unconstrained by the elitist notions of their European predecessors, they could introduce a form of playfulness to their writings.

> Pull my daisy
> tip my cup
> all my doors are open
> Cut my thoughts
> for coconuts
> all my eggs are broken
> Jack my Arden
> gate my shades
> woe my road is spoken
> Silk my garden
> rose my days
> now my prayers awaken . . .
>
>   (Ginsberg, Kerouac, and Cassady,
>   "Pull My Daisy," 1949)

For the first time in its history, America seemed on the way toward developing a uniform national identity, an official culture based on middle-class notions of propriety and success. . . .

The side streets and bars of New York City, with their ethnic subcultures and small-time criminals, kept the Beats in touch with another America, permitting the sense of being outside the mainstream and its drift to conformity. In this respect, too, the New Vision could trace its roots back to earlier periods of American cultural radicalism: Henry Miller and Ernest Hemingway in the 1920s and the proletarian writers of the 1930s rejected middle-class life-styles and sought out the downtrodden and the outsiders in a quest for authenticity and experience. By the 1940s, the political aspects of the quest had largely disappeared; what was left was the existential search for meaning and escape from the ever-growing encroachment of the official culture. Out of this search would eventually emerge the counterculture of the sixties.

A new sense of energy—as well as alienation—was expressed in Ginsberg's poems and Kerouac's novels. In Ginsberg's *After Dead Souls* (1951) and Kerouac's more famous *On the Road* (1957) the American mythology of the open road and the western frontier were reinvented for a new generation.

Where O America are you
going in your glorious
automobile, careening
down the highway
toward what crash
in the deep canyon
of the Western Rockies,
or racing the sunset
over Golden Gate
toward what wild city
jumping with jazz
on the Pacific Ocean!

(Ginsberg, "After Dead Souls," 1951)

The *Howl* Heard 'Round the World

One of the cornerstones of the New Vision was that poetry should not only deal with the everyday experience of common people but should also speak in their language. Living alone in New York and working as a free-lance market researcher, Ginsberg began in 1951 to compose the poem that was to become the anthem of a new generation. The other central subterraneans, Kerouac and Burroughs, were each on their separate roads in search of new experience. Ginsberg was thus free to return to one of his earlier sources of inspiration, namely, William Carlos Williams, one of America's most famous poets who was from a neighboring New Jersey town. He also drew on his own outsider experience, both his mother's mental illness and his own meanderings through the streets of New York. He had also, through a chance encounter with a Chinese painting at the New York Public Library, become interested in Buddhism. As already noted, the nearness of Columbia to Harlem had put Ginsberg in touch with black culture, especially jazz. Eventually all these influences would congeal into *Howl*, which combined these various strands with a powerful sense of rhythm. It was poetry that was best heard, rather than read. It seemed to require a collective presence to be fully experienced. It began with the famous lines,

> I saw the best minds of my generation destroyed by
>   madness, starving hysterical naked,
> dragging themselves through the negro streets at dawn
>   looking for an angry fix,
> angelheaded hipsters burning for ancient heavenly
>   connection to the
> starry dynamo in the machinery of night,
> who poverty and tatters and hollow-eyed and high sat up
>   smoking in
> the supernatural darkness of cold-water flats floating
>   across the tops of
> cities contemplating jazz . . .

Howl was first read publicly in San Francisco in 1955, in an event that has since taken on mythical proportions. In a room packed with all the notables of the West Coast poetry revival, Ginsberg read to the cheers and shouts of an audience of about one hundred. He filled the room with the sounds and symbols of the New Vision. As Barry Miles describes it,

> [Ginsberg] was nervous and had drunk a great deal of wine. He read with a small, intense voice, but the alcohol and the emotional intensity of the poem quickly took over, and he was soon swaying to its powerful rhythm, chanting like a

Jewish cantor, sustaining his long breath length, savoring the outrageous language. Kerouac began cheering him on, yelling "Go!" at the end of each line, and soon the audience joined in. Allen was completely transported. At each line he took a deep breath, glanced at the manuscript, then delivered it, arms outstretched, eyes gleaming, swaying from one foot to the other with the rhythm of the words. . . . Allen continued to the last sob, the audience cheering him wildly at every line. (Miles 1990)

As Kenneth Rexroth, a well-known critic and central figure in San Francisco poetry circles, said directly afterward, the poem would make Ginsberg "famous from bridge to bridge [New York City to San Francisco.]" The reading, as well as the poem itself, helped to catalyze the subterranean literary communities in New York and San Francisco. Something was indeed happening to counter the main drift in American culture. The mass media would soon help make it into a movement.

The Seeds of the Subculture

The Beats moved and drew inspiration from the marginal urban subcultural pockets and linked art and life-style together in a creative way. The underbelly of the consumer society sustained them in a material as well as a spiritual sense. But San Francisco and northern California added something else, a rural, pastoral sensibility that would connect the Beats to the ecology movement of the 1970s. . . .

Ginsberg was an important link across the generations, between the Beats and the hippies, and, less obviously, between the vague pacificism and antipolitics expressed in Beat culture and the new, direct-action politics of the 1960s. In 1963, Ginsberg took part in his first political demonstration, protesting against an appearance of Madame Nhu, the infamous Dragon Lady of [South] Vietnam, whose fierce Catholicism and religious repression had contributed, among other things, to the self-immolation of Buddhist monks. In protest, Ginsberg sang mantras for fourteen hours on the streets of San Francisco. Later in the 1960s, he acted as the forty-year-old "elder-statesman" of the political wing of the counterculture. . . . While the other key figures of the Beat generation followed a more nonpolitical road, Ginsberg helped to facilitate the transition to the new politics of the sixties. Allen Ginsberg was more than a seed of the 1960s: he was one of the most colorful flowers of the new generation.

CHAPTER 6

The Legacy
of the 1950s

The Roots of Sixties Protest

Terry H. Anderson

The 1950s are remembered as a time of conformity and political apathy while the 1960s are seen as a time of radical protest. But according to author Terry H. Anderson, the problems that existed in the sixties existed in the fifties; perhaps the fact that they had been ignored for so long caused people to react more violently when they did react. As the fifties drew to a close, issues such as segregation, nuclear testing, and anti-Communist witchhunts began to draw protest from thousands of college-age baby-boomers testing their own values and tasting independence. Leftist groups like the Students for a Democratic Society (SDS) were formed in 1960, indicating a growing moral outrage among the young.

As early as 1958, ten thousand black and white students marched in Washington, D.C., to participate in a "Youth March for Integrated Schools." The next year, twenty thousand students arrived to march. The 1955–1956 Montgomery bus boycott gave rise to the massive sit-in movement that was to follow in February 1960 when four black students sat down at a white-only Woolworth lunch counter in Greensboro, North Carolina. The students, later known as "the Greensboro 4," refused to move until they were served.

Terry H. Anderson, a Vietnam veteran, is professor of

Excerpted from *The Movement and the Sixties,* by Terry H. Anderson. Copyright ©1996 by Terry H. Anderson. Reprinted with permission from the Oxford University Press, Inc.

history at Texas A&M University. He has written several books as well as innumerable articles on the 1960s and the Vietnam war.

[The] Montgomery [bus boycott] was a beginning. While scholars debate how much that boycott prepared blacks for the subsequent civil rights crusade, it did seem to stimulate action in other locales during the last half of the decade. Blacks in Tallahassee, New Orleans, and some twenty smaller towns conducted boycotts while activists in over a dozen communities held sit-ins of some segregated businesses. These demonstrations were similar to Montgomery in that they were not led by national organizations, and if successful, they only were local victories. They did not inspire a massive civil rights movement.

That changed in February 1960 with the next stage of the black struggle, the lunch counter sit-ins [beginning in Greensboro], which were a decisive break with earlier civil rights demonstrations and with cold war culture. The sit-ins ignited a young generation of blacks to become activists, and more important, they stimulated some southern and many northern whites to participate in something they began calling "the movement."

In the weeks after the Greensboro sit-in, blacks used the college-church network to spread the news quickly throughout the South. Students started sit-ins at lunch counters in Winston-Salem, Durham, Raleigh, and other cities across North Carolina, and by the end of February activists were using the tactic in seven states and over 30 communities including Nashville, Tallahassee, Chattanooga, Richmond, and Baltimore. The stream of students sitting in during February became a flood by March and a torrent during the next months as activists employed the tactic in Charleston, Columbia, Miami, Houston, San Antonio, and even small towns such as Xenia, Ohio. Blacks also initiated new tactics against "white only" facilities, such as read-ins at public libraries, paint-ins at public art galleries, wade-ins at public beaches, kneel-ins at white churches, and in Philadelphia 400 ministers asked their congregations to boycott corporations that did not hire blacks. Throughout 1960 and the next year about 70,000 participated in thirteen states, and a newspaper in Raleigh noted that the "picket line now extends from the dime store to the United States Supreme Court and beyond that to national and world opinion."

Whites React Violently to Protest

Many southern whites reacted toward black demands for civil rights in the same manner that they had since the end of the Civil War. At first they attempted to ignore them. But the sit-in, unlike a court ruling, was impossible to disregard for it disrupted business and reduced profits. As a consequence, white officials formed committees to "study" proposals, applied pressure on older black leaders to control their youth, and demanded that black college presidents expel activists. During the first year of the sit-ins black college administrators expelled over 140 students and dismissed almost 60 faculty members.

Yet those tactics failed to stop the sit-ins, so some southerners began the unofficial response—violence. Police either conducted brutal arrests and threw thousands of peaceful black students in jail for "inciting a riot," or they looked the other way and allowed white thugs to attack. During demonstrations in Nashville white hecklers pushed lighted cigarettes into the backs of black coeds quietly sitting at the counter. They spit at black men, blew cigar smoke into their faces, and threw fried potatoes at them. They called white supporters "nigger lovers" and kicked and beat them. The demonstrators did not fight back, and when police eventually arrived they arrested scores of students, and not one assailant. In Atlanta, a white threw acid into a demonstrator's face, and during sit-ins in Houston, a white teenager slashed a black with a knife. Three others captured a protester, flogged him, carved "KKK" in his chest, and hung him by his knees from a tree. Whites in Biloxi, Mississippi, attacked blacks with clubs, chains, and guns, firing into a peaceful demonstration and wounding ten.

Repression in the past usually had worked, but during sit-ins it appalled many neutral white bystanders. When a heckler in Knoxville poured a soft drink over a black minister and then struck him in the face, a large, young white man intervened, "You fellows have gone far enough and now you'd better get out of here!" A white waitress at another store looked at the black students and said to her colleague, "I think they should be served. You know, you really have to admire their courage!"

Nor did white violence repress the demonstrations. Just the opposite: It helped young blacks form a common bond, gave them a new sense of pride, and encouraged most of them to try harder to beat segregation. They were putting their lives on the line—this time there was no turning back. These activists played a catalytic role throughout the South: They launched the 1960s.

Will Not Tolerate Discrimination

There were many reasons for this youthful activism, almost as many as there were participants, yet at the same time there were some common themes. Some had been inspired by parents, older civil rights workers, teachers, or by Martin Luther King, Jr. James Lawson, a student of theology at Vanderbilt University, reminded those engaged in Nashville sit-ins, "Remember the teachings of Jesus, Gandhi, Martin Luther King." Ezell Blair remarked that he had heard King preach two years before he joined the Greensboro sit-in, and recalled the sermon being "so strong that I could feel my heart palpitating. It brought tears to my eyes." Some students were inspired by decolonialization in Africa, where at that time a dozen nations were obtaining independence. Many others were determined to avoid what James Baldwin had predicted: "All of Africa will be free before we can get a lousy cup of coffee."

Young blacks were tired of the humiliation of discrimination, and in March 1960 students in Atlanta placed advertisements in local newspapers which explained their participation: "Every normal human being wants to walk the earth with dignity and abhors any and all proscriptions placed upon him because of race or color. In essence, this is the meaning of the sit-down protests that are sweeping this nation today." The ad warned that "Today's youth will not sit by submissively, while being denied all of the rights, privileges, and joys of life. We want to state clearly and un-equivocally that we cannot tolerate, in a nation professing democracy and among people professing Christianity, the discriminatory conditions under which the Negro is living today in Atlanta." The sit-ins, one activist wrote, were a "mass vomit against the hypocrisy of segregation."

"There is no power like the power of an idea whose time has come," wrote Thomas Paine at the beginning of the American Revolution, and to many black students in 1960 the time was Now! They were growing impatient, tired of procrastination. One of the Greensboro 4, David Rich-mond, explained that he and his companions realized "how black folks were mistreated and nobody was doing anything about it." They were tired of "many words and few deeds." These four freshmen challenged each other to do something, and the next day they began a sit-in. Two days later, after reading the paper in Atlanta, students at Morehouse College, Lonnie King and Julian Bond, dis-cussed the possibility of holding their own sit-ins at the local Woolworth's, W.T. Grant's, and Kresge's. King re-membered that his position was that the "situation in Greensboro would again be another isolated incident in black history if others didn't join in to make it become something," and that the "only people in the black com-munity at that time who were free to take on the Estab-lishment were college kids. . . ."

Idealistic American Values

These students were restless. Greensboro had demon-strated that they could challenge Jim Crow, and their ac-tions were shown every evening on television news, another reason for the awakening of a national civil rights movement. It is difficult to overestimate the importance of TV in the 1960s. Numerous authors have debated the impact of the media on the Vietnam War and antiwar movement, and one wonders if bus boycotts during the fifties would have remained local incidents if more black and white homes had televisions, or if network coverage had been more extensive. By 1960, however, Americans had purchased 50 million TVs, and during the next years the network evening news expanded from fifteen minutes to half an hour. With more extensive coverage virtually every citizen could witness—and judge—the Southern Way of Life. "With the exception of the announcer's voice," black student Cleveland Sellers said, "the lounge would be so quiet you could hear a rat pissing on cotton. Hundreds of thoughts coursed through my head as I stood with my eyes transfixed on the television screen. My identification with the demonstrating students was so thorough that I would flinch every time one of the whites taunted them. On nights when I saw pictures of students being beaten and dragged through the streets by their hair, I would leave the lounge in a rage." Television not only provoked southern blacks to join the movement; it stimulated those residing in the North. As Robert Moses watched his set in Harlem he realized it was time to act: "They were kids my own age and I knew this had something to do with my life."

Student participation and leadership in 1960 set a pattern for the movement during the entire decade. Students were ideal protesters since compared with the rest of society they had little to lose. They usually did not have responsibilities such as families or careers, and often had more free time and more energy. Also, black students and ministers, unlike most blacks in the South in 1960, were relatively organized in colleges or congregations, and neither depended on the white society for their economic livelihood. When students or ministers demonstrated they could not be fired from their jobs; both could afford to fight Jim Crow.

Young activists in the early 1960s, both black and white, also had fewer concrete notions about what was possible and impossible, and they were more idealistic. Raised in cold war culture, their teachers had them memorize the words of the Constitution—"we the people"—and the Declaration of Independence—"all men are created equal." Yet such words rang hollow in the South. As Tom Hayden stated about his years as a civil rights worker, "We were imbued with very idealistic American values: a belief in racial integration, not just as a future ideal, but as an ideal to be practiced in the here and now; a belief that places like Mississippi were not part of the American dream, but nightmares that America would awaken from; a belief, finally, that the Constitution, the president, and the American people were really on our side. Our example would mobilize them."

"For the first time in our history," wrote a professor in the early 1960s, "a major social movement, shaking the nation to its bones, is being led by youngsters.". . .

The sit-ins continued in 1961 and by the end of that year the students had achieved impressive results. Activists had integrated lunch counters and theaters in Greensboro and nearly 200 other cities, including larger ones such as Houston and Atlanta. Success was contagious: more black and white students joined the movement, and that provoked participation from parents and many prominent blacks, such as Sidney Poitier, Harry Belafonte, and Sammy Davis, Jr. Comedian Dick Gregory led many sit-ins, and when whites told him, "We don't serve Negroes," he responded, "No problem, I don't eat Negroes."

Northern politicians spoke out in favor of civil rights, and so did some progressive southerners such as Frank P. Graham, former senator and president of the University of North Carolina, who proclaimed that black protesters were renewing the nation: "In sitting down they are standing up for the American dream." Black students had demonstrated in little over a year that change was possible, that some whites would accept integrated public facilities.

The Southern Way of Life was not impregnable. Success also was exhilarating. "I walked the picket line and I sat in," said one activist, "and the walls of segregation toppled. . . . Nothing can stop us now. . . ."

White Students Organize on Campus

Students also became concerned with other issues after the McCarthy era. The bomb, and the atomic fear it produced, was critical in the late fifties since atmospheric testing resulted in traces of radioactivity in the nation's food supply and dairy products. A number of older peace activists responded by organizing the National Committee for a SANE Nuclear Policy, commonly called SANE. Some students joined SANE or Peacemakers, a group opposed to civil defense drills "since one H-bomb would end New York City." During spring semester 1960 a thousand Harvard students held a protest walk for nuclear disarmament, and three months after Greensboro hundreds of students participated with over 15,000 older citizens in a rally at Madison Square Garden aimed at ending the nuclear arms race and creating a test ban treaty. Peacemakers attributed the big turnout to the fact that "many students are now aware of and responding to an atmosphere of action resulting from the Southern sit-ins."

On campus, students began organizing or joining groups such as Turn Toward Peace, Committee for Nonviolent Action, the Student Peace Union, and they began publishing dissident journals and magazines such as *New University Thought* (Chicago), *New Freedom* (Cornell), *Studies on the Left* (Wisconsin), *Advance* (Harvard), *The Activist* (Oberlin), and *Alternatives* (Illinois). During the next two years over 25 of these journals appeared on almost 20 campuses. Some students also formed political parties concerned with civil rights, academic freedom, or campus issues. . . .

On a few select campuses, then, the spring of 1960 witnessed the first pulse of student activism, and it troubled the older generation who remained steeped in cold war culture. The government responded in May 1960. HUAC

[House Un-American Activities Committee] held hearings in the Bay Area to investigate "Communist activities." That prompted a thousand Berkeley students to protest the investigations at city hall in San Francisco. The first day of the demonstration was peaceful, but not the second day. Students were singing "the land of the free, home of the brave," when police appeared with billy clubs and fire hoses, drenching the protesters. As Betty Denitch remembered, "Here were students being dragged by their hair, dragged by their arms and legs down the stairs so that their heads were bouncing off the stairs." Students labeled the affair "Black Friday," and Denitch later stated: "That was the start of the sixties for me. . . ."

Other students volunteered for tasks in campus organizations. The Student Peace Union only had 150 members in 1960 but boasted 4000 three years later. SANE also expanded, and the Young People's Socialist League tripled to 800 by 1962. By the standards of the 1950s, these organizations were "radical" because they no longer were afraid to state their views at a small demonstration; by the standards of the late 1960s, however, these were little more than debating societies. [Harvard College political action committee] TOCSIN activities were the "most gentlemanly form of protest imaginable," one member remembered, "based on the assumption that a rational dialogue between Harvard faculty and Harvard students would save the world from destruction." Yet compared with the fifties, any dialogue seemed an improvement to young activists like Todd Gitlin, who stated his reason for becoming involved: "TOCSIN made me feel useful, gave me good company, books to read, intellectual energy."

The Youthful Idealism of John F. Kennedy Signaled the End of the 1950s

Peter Joseph

The fifties drew to a close along with the presidency of the aging Republican Dwight D. Eisenhower. Americans elected Democrat John F. Kennedy to office in 1960; at the time, the forty-three-year-old Kennedy was the youngest chief executive in American history. His presidency was a potent symbol: Eisenhower, the conservative World War II general born in 1890, passed the torch to a vibrant, savvy idealist at the dawn of the sixties.

Peter Joseph, a graduate of Princeton University, was awarded the Dewitt Clinton Poole Prize and the Woodrow Wilson Prize for Senior Thesis of Unusual Merit for his essay about Kennedy and the idealism he inspired in others.

The boom in the private sector during the 1950s left much of America in a state of seemingly secure affluence, but the nation's public spirit simultaneously plummeted to dangerous depths. There was that great race for membership in the middle class, and more than ever a person's accumulation of material goods measured his standing in society. Americans tunneled their vision and worked hard at getting ahead. After the rollicking Twenties, the Depression-dominated Thirties, and the war in the Forties,

---

Excerpted from *Good Times: An Oral History of America in the 1960s,* by Peter Joseph, (New York: Morrow, 1974). Copyright ©1973 by Peter Joseph. Reprinted with permission from the author.

America had seemed glad to sit back in the easy chair, slippered feet on the ottoman and eyes riveted to the television set, guzzling a sparkling Budweiser. Then, perhaps tired of the fat Roman life, and perhaps fearing a fall, the people listened to the call of John Fitzgerald Kennedy.

When John Kennedy set out in early 1960 to win the Presidency, he exhibited a different brand of leadership. He was young, attractive, daring, and eager for power—traits that most Americans coveted and admired. He surrounded himself with men of intellect and culture, [who were known as the] New Frontiersmen. He infused in Americans a new sense of pride in their nation and an eagerness to share in the long agenda of unfinished business before them. He so ignited his countrymen that they cheered—they even came to revere—the admonition, "Ask not what your country can do for you. Ask what you can do for your country." One has to go back to Theodore Roosevelt and earlier, to the days of the Revolution, to find the national leadership in the hands of such idealistic and daring young men.

By the late 1950s television had linked the nation in a continental living room, giving the man in the White House an unprecedented power to radiate a mood and a sense of purpose. Dwight D. Eisenhower chose not to exercise this enormous power to rally the nation behind a social program. John Kennedy chose to use all that power. The great cliché of the period was that Kennedy was far more image than substance, that he got by largely on a kind of show-business charisma, that he was at least as much celebrity as political leader. One can accept or reject that evaluation of the man, but it is true that, whatever the substance of his achievement, he *did* affect the national consciousness in a remarkable and stirring fashion. The Kennedy Presidency unleashed enormous energy and passion in vast sectors of the populace, especially in those sectors in which the people had been least powerful and least successful in sharing the fruits of the American Dream.

Kennedy was able to understand and empathize with the young, who were so taken by him that they quickly rallied

At age forty-four, John F. Kennedy was the youngest man elected president. Daring, intelligent, and charismatic, Kennedy's election signaled the beginning of a new era in American history.

around his banner. He excited them when he spoke with his nicely cadenced, crisply articulated, unbloated brand of patriotism. Their idealism and his meshed: to the President and to the young alike the hypocrisy evident in the gap between the American credo and the American practice became fair game for reform. The Peace Corps ideally embodied this new sense of mission. The Office of Economic Opportunity, incorporating VISTA [Volunteers in Service to America] as the domestic Peace Corps, would later work in the same manner. Once unleashed, the young were not to be halted by the blows and harassment that came rain-ing down on them as the decade wore on, though the dreams of many would soon lose their glow.

In President Kennedy the blacks found a man in charge of the national government who was committed to ending their degraded state. Though the Supreme Court had outlawed segregation in 1954, President Eisenhower had declined to speak out with any moral fervor on the matter. The Kennedys spoke out. Attorney General Robert F. Kennedy ordered the Interstate Commerce Commission to force the desegregation of interstate transportation facilities in November of 1962. The President personally stood up to the effrontery of Governors Ross Barnett [of Mississippi] and George Wallace [of Alabama], thus forcing the integration of the Universities of Mississippi and Alabama. During his showdown with Governor Wallace in June 1963, Kennedy asked a nationwide television audience:

> Are we to say to the world—and much more importantly to each other—that this is the land of the free except for the Negroes; that we have no second-class citizens except Negroes; that we have no class or caste system, no ghettos, no master race, except with respect to Negroes?

Reaching out for the understanding and conscience of America, Kennedy sought to soften the hardened hearts of a nation that might have rendered meaningless the laws to come. With such a powerful ally rallying the nation to their cause, black Americans began themselves to lead the fight for long-delayed equality. And in that fight they made remarkable progress.

The Origins of Environmental Awareness

Rachel Carson

From the development of plastics to medical miracles such as the polio vaccine, in the 1950s it seemed no problem could not be solved by science. But people soon found that scientific and technological wonders came with a price.

The pesticide known as DDT (dichloro-diphenyl-trichloroethane) was at first considered another fifties marvel. The chemical attacked the nervous systems of harmful insects such as flies, lice, and mosquitoes but seemed to have little observable affect on warm-blooded mammals (like humans). And it was cheap to manufacture. House-wives were advised to spray DDT in their kitchens, bathrooms, mattresses, and even on family pets to get rid of bedbugs, lice, ticks, and cockroaches. DDT quickly became one of the world's most widely used chemicals.

DDT, however, also kills beneficial insects like bees along with dozens of bird species that eat DDT-tainted insects. In addition, the chemical breaks down very slowly, and scientists began to notice accumulations of the pesticide in the fatty tissues of some farm animals. Cows that ate grass sprayed with DDT passed the chemical along to humans, especially women. Nursing mothers passed it along to their infants.

Rachel Carson, best-selling author of the 1951 book *The*

Sea Around Us, began to research the harmful side effects of DDT in the late 1950s. The outcry that followed her 1962 book, *Silent Spring,* spurred revolutionary changes in laws affecting the land, water, and air and was instrumental in launching the environmental movement.

The history of life on earth has been a history of interaction between living things and their surroundings. . . . Only within the moment of time represented by the present century has one species—man—acquired significant power to alter the nature of his world.

During the past quarter century this power has not only increased to one of disturbing magnitude but it has changed in character. The most alarming of all man's assaults upon the environment is the contamination of air, earth, rivers, and sea with dangerous and even lethal materials. This pollution is for the most part irrecoverable; the chain of evil it initiates not only in the world that must support life but in living tissues is for the most part irreversible. In this now universal contamination of the environment, chemicals are the sinister and little-recognized partners of radiation in changing the very nature of the world—the very nature of its life. Strontium 90, released through nuclear explosions into the air, comes to earth in rain or drifts down as fallout, lodges in soil, enters into the grass or corn or wheat grown there, and in time takes up its abode in the bones of a human being, there to remain until his death. Similarly, chemicals sprayed on croplands or forests or gardens lie long in soil, entering into living organisms, passing from one to another in a chain of poisoning and death. Or they pass mysteriously by underground streams until they emerge and, through the alchemy of air and sunlight, combine into new forms that kill vegetation, sicken cattle, and work unknown harm on those who drink from once pure wells. As Albert Schweitzer has said, "Man can hardly even recognize the devils of his own creation."

"Unnatural Creations of Man's Tampering"

It took hundreds of millions of years to produce the life that now inhabits the earth—eons of time in which that developing and evolving and diversifying life reached a state of adjustment and balance with its surroundings. The environment, rigorously shaping and directing the life it supported, contained elements that were hostile as well as supporting. Certain rocks gave out dangerous radiation; even within the light of the sun, from which all life draws its energy, there were short-wave radiations with power to injure. Given time—time not in years but in millennia—life adjusts, and a balance has been reached. For time is the essential ingredient; but in the modern world there is no time.

The rapidity of change and the speed with which new situations are created follow the impetuous and heedless pace of man rather than the deliberate pace of nature. Radiation is no longer merely the background radiation of rocks, the bombardment of cosmic rays, the ultraviolet of the sun that have existed before there was any life on earth; radiation is now the unnatural creation of man's tampering with the atom. The chemicals to which life is asked to make its adjustment are no longer merely the calcium and silica and copper and all the rest of the minerals washed out of the rocks and carried in rivers to the sea; they are the synthetic creations of man's inventive mind, brewed in his laboratories, and having no counterparts in nature.

To adjust to these chemicals would require time on the scale that is nature's; it would require not merely the years of a man's life but the life of generations. And even this, were it by some miracle possible, would be futile, for the new chemicals come from our laboratories in an endless stream; almost five hundred annually find their way into actual use in the United States alone. The figure is staggering and its implications are not easily grasped—500 new chemicals to which the bodies of men and animals are required somehow to adapt each year, chemicals totally outside the limits of biologic experience.

Two Hundred New Chemicals for Killing Pests

Among them are many that are used in man's war against nature. Since the mid-1940's over 200 basic chemicals have been created for use in killing insects, weeds, rodents, and other organisms described in the modern vernacular as "pests"; and they are sold under several thousand different brand names.

These sprays, dusts, and aerosols are now applied almost universally to farms, gardens, forests, and homes—nonselective chemicals that have the power to kill every insect, the "good" and the "bad," to still the song of birds and the leaping of fish in the streams, to coat the leaves with a deadly film, and to linger on in soil—all this though the intended target may be only a few weeds or insects. Can anyone believe it is possible to lay down such a barrage of poisons on the surface of the earth without making it unfit for all life? They should not be called "insecticides," but "biocides."

The whole process of spraying seems caught up in an endless spiral. Since DDT was released for civilian use, a process of escalation has been going on in which ever more toxic materials must be found. This has happened because insects, in a triumphant vindication of Darwin's principle of the survival of the fittest, have evolved super races immune to the particular insecticide used, hence a deadlier one has always to be developed—and then a deadlier one than that. It has happened also because, for reasons to be described later, destructive insects often undergo a "flareback," or resurgence, after spraying, in numbers greater than before. Thus the chemical war is never won, and all life is caught in its violent crossfire.

Contamination of the Total Environment

Along with the possibility of the extinction of mankind by nuclear war, the central problem of our age has therefore become the contamination of man's total environment with such substances of incredible potential for harm—substances that accumulate in the tissues of plants and animals and even penetrate the germ cells to shatter or alter the very material of heredity upon which the shape of the future depends.

Some would-be architects of our future look toward a time when it will be possible to alter the human germ plasm by design. But we may easily be doing so now by inadvertence, for many chemicals, like radiation, bring about

Environmentalist and author Rachel Carson (pictured) warned the public about the dangers of using DDT.

gene mutations. It is ironic to think that man might determine his own future by something so seemingly trivial as the choice of an insect spray.

All this has been risked—for what? Future historians may well be amazed by our distorted sense of proportion. How could intelligent beings seek to control a few unwanted species by a method that contaminated the entire environment and brought the threat of disease and death even to their own kind?

Yet this is precisely what we have done. We have done it, moreover, for reasons that collapse the moment we examine them. We are told that the enormous and expanding use of pesticides is necessary to maintain farm production. Yet is our real problem not one of *overproduction?* Our farms, despite measures to remove acreages from production and to pay farmers *not* to produce, have yielded such a staggering excess of crops that the American taxpayer in 1962 is paying out more than one billion dollars a year as the total carrying cost of the surplus-food storage program. And is the situation helped when one branch of the Agriculture Department tries to reduce production while another states, as it did in 1958, "It is believed generally that reduction of crop acreages under provisions of the Soil Bank will stimulate interest in use of chemicals to obtain maximum production on the land retained in crops."

All this is not to say there is no insect problem and no need of control. I am saying, rather, that control must be geared to realities, not to mythical situations, and that the methods employed must be such that they do not destroy us along with the insects. . . .

Developed for Chemical Warfare

For the first time in the history of the world, every human being is now subjected to contact with dangerous chemicals, from the moment of conception until death. In the less than two decades of their use, the synthetic pesticides have been so thoroughly distributed throughout the animate and inanimate world that they occur virtually everywhere. They have been recovered from most of the major river systems and even from streams of groundwater flowing unseen through the earth. Residues of these chemicals linger in soil to which they may have been applied a dozen years before. They have entered and lodged in the bodies of fish, birds, reptiles, and domestic and wild animals so universally that scientists carrying on animal experiments find it almost impossible to locate subjects free from such contamination. They have been found in fish in remote mountain lakes, in earthworms burrowing in soil, in the eggs of birds—and in man himself. For these chemicals are now stored in the bodies of the vast majority of human beings, regardless of age. They occur in the mother's milk, and probably in the tissues of the unborn child.

All this has come about because of the sudden rise and prodigious growth of an industry for the production of man-made or synthetic chemicals with insecticidal properties. This industry is a child of the Second World War. In the course of developing agents of chemical warfare, some of the chemicals created in the laboratory were found to be lethal to insects. The discovery did not come by chance: insects were widely used to test chemicals as agents of death for man.

The result has been a seemingly endless stream of synthetic insecticides. In being man-made—by ingenious laboratory manipulation of the molecules, substituting atoms, altering their arrangement—they differ sharply from the simpler insecticides of prewar days. These were derived from naturally occurring minerals and plant products—compounds of arsenic, copper, lead, manganese, zinc, and other minerals, pyrethrum from the dried flowers of chrysanthemums, nicotine sulphate from some of the relatives of tobacco, and rotenone from leguminous plants of the East Indies.

Disrupting Vital Body Processes

What sets the new synthetic insecticides apart is their enormous biological potency. They have immense power not merely to poison but to enter into the most vital processes of the body and change them in sinister and often deadly ways. Thus, as we shall see, they destroy the very enzymes whose function is to protect the body from harm, they block the oxidation processes from which the body receives its energy, they prevent the normal functioning of various organs, and they may initiate in certain cells the slow and irreversible change that leads to malignancy.

Yet new and more deadly chemicals are added to the list each year and new uses are devised so that contact with these materials has become practically worldwide. The production of synthetic pesticides in the United States soared from 124,259,000 pounds in 1947 to 637,666,000 pounds in 1960—more than a fivefold increase. The wholesale value of these products was well over a quarter of a billion dollars. But in the plans and hopes of the industry this enormous production is only a beginning.

Chronology

1950

Census shows 150,697,361 people living in the United States.

January 31—President Harry Truman approves production of the hydrogen bomb.

February 9—Senator Joseph McCarthy claims many in federal government are Communists. This speech ushers in four years of Red-baiting later known as the McCarthy era.

June 27—Truman sends air force and navy personnel to Korea after North Korea invades the south. Ground forces are sent three days later.

November 26—Chinese troops attack UN forces in Korea.

1951

Employment of women reaches peak of 19.3 million.

Supreme Court bars "subversives" from teaching in public schools.

March 29—Julius and Ethel Rosenberg found guilty of selling U.S. atomic secrets to the Soviet Union; they are sentenced to death.

July—Korea cease-fire talks begin and last two years.

September 4—Transcontinental television begins with a speech by Truman.

1952

TV Guide magazine is founded.

November 1—The first hydrogen bomb is exploded by the United States.

November 4—Dwight D. Eisenhower is elected president.

1953

The Soviet Union tests its first hydrogen bomb.

Earl Warren appointed chief justice of Supreme Court, ushering in an era of court-ordered civil rights victories for African Americans.

March 5—Soviet dictator Joseph Stalin dies.

June 19—Ethel and Julius Rosenberg die in the electric chair.

July 27—Fighting ends in Korea.

1954
Nuclear fallout problem widely debated.

January 21—The first atomic-powered submarine, *Nautilus,* is launched in Groton, Connecticut.

May 17—Supreme Court orders school desegregation and declares separate-but-equal-schools unconstitutional in landmark case, *Brown v. Board of Education.*

April 22—McCarthy begins nationally televised hearings on Communist infiltration of the U.S. Army, which initiate McCarthy's downfall.

December 22—Senate votes 67–22 to censure McCarthy for his behavior during the Army-McCarthy hearings.

1955
United States formally ends World War II–era occupation of Germany.

First presidential press conference filmed for TV.

Salk polio vaccine is developed.

Bill Haley and the Comets have number-one hit with "Rock Around the Clock."

Tranquilizers come into widespread use.

May 31—Supreme Court orders public schools integrated with "all deliberate speed."

September 30—Actor James Dean is killed in a car accident.

December 1—Rosa Parks refuses to give up her seat to a white person on a Montgomery, Alabama, bus. Her arrest sparks a boycott that results in the abolition of segregation and Jim Crow laws in that city.

1956

January 30—Martin Luther King Jr. urges nonviolence after his house is firebombed during the Montgomery bus boycott.

March 12—More than one hundred U.S. congressmen call for resistance to Supreme Court–ordered desegregation.

April 21—Elvis Presley has first number-one hit with "Heartbreak Hotel."

June 29—Federal Highway Act is signed marking the beginning of an extensive interstate highway building program.

1957

Jack Kerouac publishes *On the Road.*

April 29—Voting rights are confirmed for African Americans when Congress passes a civil rights bill.

September 4—Arkansas National Guardsmen prevent nine black children from entering Little Rock's Central High.

September 24—Eisenhower sends federal troops to Arkansas to provide safe passage into Central High for the Little Rock Nine.

October 4—Soviet Union launches *Sputnik,* the first man-made satellite.

1958

Nikita Khrushchev becomes premier of Soviet Union.

January 31—First U.S. satellite, *Explorer,* successfully orbits the earth.

March 24—Elvis Presley enters the U.S. Army.

December 10—The first domestic jet-airline passenger service begins between New York City and Miami.

1959

January 1—Fidel Castro becomes dictator of Cuba.

January 3—Alaska becomes the forty-ninth state.

August 21—Hawaii becomes the fiftieth state.

September 15–27—Nikita Khrushchev visits the United States, but is barred from going to Disneyland for security reasons.

For Further Reading

Paul Boyer, *By the Bomb's Early Light: American Thought and Culture at the Dawn of the Atomic Age*. New York: Pantheon, 1985.

Rachel Carson, *Silent Spring*. Boston: Houghton Mifflin, 1962.

Editors of Time-Life Books, *Rock and Roll Generation*. Richmond, VA: Time-Life Books, 1998.

David Honeyboy Edwards (as told to Janis Martinson and Michael Robert Frank), *The World Don't Owe Me Nothing*. Chicago: Chicago Review Press, 1997.

Warren French, *San Francisco Poetry Renaissance: 1955–1960*. Boston: Twayne, 1991.

David Halberstam, *The Fifties*. New York: Villard, 1993.

Henry Hampton and Steve Fayer, *Voices of Freedom*. New York: Bantam, 1990.

Brett Harvey, *The Fifties: A Woman's Oral History*. New York: HarperCollins, 1993.

Walter L. Hixton, *Parting the Curtain: Propaganda, Culture, and the Cold War*. New York: St. Martin's Press, 1997.

Jack Kerouac, *On the Road*. New York: Viking, 1957.

J. Fred MacDonald, *One Nation Under Television*. New York: Pantheon, 1990.

Karal Ann Marling, *As Seen on TV*. Cambridge, MA: Harvard University Press, 1994.

Douglas T. Miller and Marion Nowak, *The Fifties: The Way We Really Were*. Garden City, NY: Doubleday, 1975.

Rosa Parks (with Gregory J. Reed), *Quiet Strength*. Grand Rapids, MI: Zondervan, 1994.

I.F. Stone, *The Haunted Fifties*. New York: Random House, 1969.

David P. Szatmary, *Rockin' in Time: A Social History of Rock and Roll*. Englewood Cliffs, NJ:Prentice-Hall, 1987.

Index